AF652765

EDUCATION AND HEALTH PROBLEMS IN TRIBAL DEVELOPMENT

EDUCATION AND HEALTH PROBLEMS IN TRIBAL DEVELOPMENT

(A Study of National Integration)

Edited by

KANCHAN ROY

CONCEPT PUBLISHING COMPANY NEW DELHI - 110059

All rights reserved. No part of this work may be reproduced, stored in a retrieval system or transmitted in any form or by any means, electronic, mechanical, photocopying, micro-filming, recording or otherwise, without the prior written permission of the copyright owner and the publisher.

ISBN : 81-7022-236-2

2008

© Kanchan Roy (*b* 1952-)

Published and Printed by
Ashok Kumar Mittal
Concept Publishing Company
A/15-16, Commercial Block, Mohan Garden
New Delhi-110059 (India)

Phones : 25351460, 25351794
Fax : 091-11-25357109
Email : publishing@conceptpub.com
website: www.conceptpub.com

DEDICATED

TO

Late. Professor (Dr) L.P. Vidyarthi

Head and Director,

Centre For Advance Study In Anthropology,

&

Postgraduate Department of Anthropology,

Ranchi University, Ranchi.

PREFACE

Late Professor L.P. Vidyarthi was a scholar of many faceted interests. He was constantly in search of newer fields to which anthropologists could contribute. The year 1985 was a quite troublesome in Indian history domestically. During this year we came to know about the various political/territorial disintegration movements in some of the quarters of our country. Chotanagpur was no exception. Professor Vidyarthi with his patriotic fervour and research zeal was thinking in the line of 'what ails Chotanagpur'? He was inquisitive in the areas of tribal development works being executed in the area, the feedback system being adopted by administrators or planners, the folk view of the existing opportunities in various fields and the attempt being made to the sensitive area of harmonious national integration. Having these broad areas in mind and to get an insight to the problem direct from the persons related to the fields, he was planning seminars at National level in various zones of the country. As a first endeavour to this project the Ranchi chapter was inaugurated through one day seminar on 12 October, 1985 on the theme National Integration and Tribal Development. It was under joint collaboration of Centre for Advance Study in Anthropology, Ranchi University with the Institute of Bio-Social Research (IBRAD) Calcutta. The seminar was divided into a number of sessions dealing with 1) Education and Value System, 2) Tribal Health and Medicine, 3) Area Development and 4) Tribal Economy. It is beyond doubt that the seminar was grand success and well attended. The Judicial Commissioner, Justice A.P. Sinha, was the Chief guest and inaugurated the seminar. Many VIPs, such as Tribal Development Commissioner, Rural Development Commissioner, Pro-Vice Chancellor, Administrators and famous social scientists of the Eastern Zone actively participated by presenting their views.

The most tragic part of the story is that within two months of this seminar of National Importance we lost Professor Vidyarthi untimely and this one happened to be Dr. Vidyarthi's last attended seminar. As a programme co-ordinator of that seminar, I felt the responsibility of getting the contents published because of my emotional attachment with him as a colleague and also because of the national importance of the theme and uniqueness of the approach to the problem. As most of the editors face in this country, that the papers presented to the seminar are not submitted in due time for publication and due to that some important themes could not be included through presented papers such as on Tribal Economy and to some extent the Area Development. I hope to include those in the forthcoming editions of the book. I have kept all articles in their original form and most of the papers have suggestions to the problems they have studied . Thus the book will certainly be of much interest to a wide range of readers such as students, teachers, researchers of Tribal Welfare, Anthropology, Sociology, Social Work and Allied Disciplines, Administrators, Planners, Politicians, Voluntary agencies engaged in tribal upliftment works and others alike.

I am thankful to (Late) Professor Vidyarthi (to whom this volume is dedicated posthumously) for appointing me the Programme Coordinator for the seminar and encouraging me constantly for its grand success even in his sick bed.

I am thankful to Shri. S.B. Roy, Chairman, IBRAD, Calcutta for collaborating with our Department and Ranchi JAYCEES for extending their nice hospitality to the participants, and for the photographs.

Last but not the least, I am grateful to the publishers for being very kind to understand the importance of the work and agreeing to publish this historical happening in the anthropological scene for the cause of the Nation.

Centre for Advance Study in Anthropology
Postgraduate Department of Anthropology
Ranchi University, Ranchi (Bihar)

Kanchan Roy

CONTENTS

CONTRIBUTORS

SUNIL ARORA
Department of Anthropology, Ranchi, Bihar-834001.

L. N. BHAGAT
Postgraduate Department of Economics, Ranchi University, Ranchi-834008

A. K. CHOUDHURY
Anthropological Survey of India, 27-Jawaharlal Nehru Road, Calcutta-700016.

D. CHOUDHURY
Anthropological Survey of India, 27 Jawaharlal Nehru Road, Calcutta-700016.

S. P. GUPTA
J. P. Institute of Social Studies, Circular Road, Lalpur, Ranchi.

M. HAQUE
Anthropological Survey of India, 27 Jawaharlal Nehru Road, Calcutta-700016

M. H. R. KHASHMISI
Anthropological Survey of India, 27 Jawaharlal Nehru Road, Calcutta-700016.

S. K. PAL
Anthropological Survey of India, 27 Jawaharlal Nehru Road, Calcutta-700016

KANCHAN ROY
Postgraduate Department of Anthropology, Ranchi University, Ranchi.

B. N. SAHAY
Centre for Advance Study in Anthropology, Anthropology Department, Ranchi University, Ranchi.

K. N. SAHAY
Centre for Advance Study in Anthropology, Anthropology Department, Ranchi University, Ranchi.

A. N. SANDHWAR
Postgraduate Department of Anthropology, Ranchi University, Ranchi.

A. K. SINHA
Postgraduate Department of Anthropology, Ranchi University, Ranchi.

ANAND PRASAD SINHA
Patna High Court, Patna.

The Editor addressing the seminar

Chief guest Justice Sinha delivering
the inaugural address.

ONE

The Framework and Tribal Problems

Kanchan Roy

India has been the abode of many ethno-cultural varieties of population through prehistoric and historic times. We can trace back human presence upto 1,00,00 years, B.C. till date. India's uniqueness lies in her great assimilating power which has resulted in the rich mosaic of multi-ethnic and cultural heritage of the present. Many population groups have been inhabiting side by side through centuries without much conflict and interference in the enjoyment of one's socio-economic niches.

Now, India has become the motherland of 700 million people and 7% of which are Tribals. Though it is very difficult to define a tribe scientifically for academic purpose but viewing the temporal antiquity, spatial isolation, historical past, level of techno-economic development and *'way out'* socio-political and cultural elements, the Government of India has specified 427 communities and has included them in the schedule of tribes. These scheduled tribes are entitled to special protection and privileges under the Constitution of India. Though they have been given an uniform status of tribals but the actual situation is much complex, because these groups of people differ in socio-cultural, demographic, ecological and economical areas with one another. Demographically their numbers though have increased to 41.09 million from 19.17 million (1951 census) but some are in lakhs (Gonds, Bhils, Santhals, Mundas and Oraons) whereas some are to bare 23 souls living in the Andamans (the Great Andamanese). The present day geographical distribution is also heterogeneous. The Union territories of Andaman and Nicobar Islands, Lakshadweep, Mizoram and Arunachal Pradesh have around 80% of their populations as tribals. Among states, Madhya Pradesh has the maximum tribal concentration followed by Orissa, Bihar, Maharashtra, Gujarat, Rajasthan and West Bengal. Though these groups of people have a basic primitive subsistence economy but can be traced to various levels of development in the National stream. Some are hunters/gatherers and fruit collectors, others shifting cultivators or settled agriculturists, yet others are Industrial labourers and educated youths with white collar jobs. However, in general their economic aspects and the standard of living is depressingly low. They are among the lowest rung of development in comparison to other communities in terms of income, social status, educational level, housing and sanitary conditions and standard of health.

It is going to be forty years of our independence and Government of India under series of plans initiated special schemes for the development of tribal areas to supplement the benefits accruing from general programmes of development in different fields such as i) communication, ii) education and culture, iii) development of tribal economy, and iv) health, housing and water supply. Some plans have also been divided according to sponsorship, Central Government or by the States. To carry out these programmes, tribal development blocks were established on the lines of community development blocks. They were constituted in a tribal inhabited area of concentrations of 25,000 persons. The second plan advocated the establishment of 40 multipurpose pilot projects in the plan period for intensive and coordinated development with slight modifications. The Integrated Area Development has been a step further where Micro, Meso and Macro areas having clearly defined objectives were also set up.

Though none can ignore the genuine desire of the Government to uplift the tribal people and its efforts in changing the mode of thinking and attitude of many tribals but inspite of this the efforts so far have not helped in solving their problems of the poverty, malnutrition and exploitation. It is said that the impact of the educational programmes of the Government has been uneven. Only few selected tribes have been benefitted and reservations have created much problem in service. The tribal development blocks have failed to do their tasks and the benefits failed to reach the lower strata of the society, The upper crust of the tribal community had it in their hands. The plans were inconsistent with the social, cultural and ecological/environmental needs of the tribals. Industrialization and urbanisation created a lot of problems for the tribals. They are forced to abandon their villages and as a result migration towards heterogeneous environment is taking place and they are getting their places in urban slums losing their sense of identity. No attempts have been made to involve tribal people themselves in the implementation of programmes to ascertain their requirements. There are structural anomalies in the tribal development administration also including technical procedure of fund transfer, inappropriate delegation of power, politicization of true workers or administrators, the availability of fund and varying nature of fund allocation, bureaucratic apathy and red tapism. The Integrated area development plan is criticised that if successful it can only make a few tribes viable farmers/enterpreneurs or service class members while a large number of the tribals will remain where they were or can be pushed to a worse plight. Views are there that the tribals have failed to lead in such collective projects and the voluntary organizations under Government protege can work to certain extent but conferring economic power to them may lead to exploitation of poor instead. It is apparent that most of the plans have been a failure mostly due to the inadequate knowledge about the tribals, the specific needs of the ecology, economy and society and their developmental requisitions.

It is some of these points where anthropologists can contribute through their field work starting from micro or village level to the macro or urban level in terms of short term and long term planning. The papers presented in the book may give one an idea about the practical problems faced by the tribals in the areas of education and their value system, their health and nutrition and development. Some of the papers herein have tried to trace the gap between the tribal cognition and the 'main stream' culture of Indian society in general.

Justice A.P. Sinha, Judicial Commissioner, in his presidential address puts forward his observation on the tribals of Chotanagpur. He noticed that the elements of superstition is to such an extent that the murders are quite often committed with the notion of witchcraft. According to him the present system of education has no meaning to the tribal youths. They very soon become drop outs which make them unemployeds or misfit for any jobs. Gradually they are taken to the anti-social activities. He also blames the local or tribal leaders in this area, who are there for selfish gains or 'personal development' and least interested in tribal development. While concluding he believes in all-round development of the tribals because they are the integral part of the our highly mosaic society.

In his keynote address on education and value system Professor K.N. Sahay sees education and value system as two sides of a coin. He begins with the aims of education and various forms of it. While tracing the historical aspect of education in this country he opposes British System and looks forward to have some Indian elements inculcating traditional values such as concepts of Dharma etc., in our education enhancing our civilizational traditions. Though it is difficult to regulate culture through informal education but it can be helpful in neutralizing negative influences to some extent. According to him Cinema, Radio and Television can be the media for the dissemination of both formal and informal education. He does not ignore the role of family and socio-cultural life which happens to be the first school of human beings. Tribal folklores, riddles, tales, youth dormitories did inculcate the values as truthfulness, honesty and integrity through times immemorial. Schools should also preach morality through effective communication.

B.N. Sahay understands education in terms of social values, economic upliftment, health, culture and spiritual development. He brings out the faults underlying the present educational system and suggests some ways of innovation in the fields of economy, health and spiritual development.

Focussing on university education among the tribals, Anil Kishore Sinha, presents his survey report related to the problems of Ranchi University tribal students. While concluding, he suggests some innovative points which may prove to be useful if they are followed.

Sushil Arora points out the possibility of an important role which could be played by the audio-visual media in tribal development and National Integration. He sketches the status of the three audio-visual media, the Television, Cinema and Video of India and Bihar in particular. He sees Indian cinema and T.V. as a good example of unity in diversity in terms of organizational structure. Some programmes of 'Doordarshan' and contents of cinema and videos do have the themes of National integration and had been very popular. All these instil a sense of "we" feeling. His valuable suggestions may be of interest to the persons in the allied fields.

L.N. Bhagat in his case study on Oraons and Kharia tribes of Chotanagpur makes education a central theme. He begins with a hypothesis that low literacy rate and educational status generally make the tribals unaware of developmental plans offered by government and other agencies. Christianity in Chotanagpur region has brought in higher educational scores, higher value orientation but considerably lower average annual income as compared to the Non-Christian Oraons. Their values have been shifted to more leisure loving attitudes. He also finds a high positive correlation between educational status and value orientation, on one hand and positive association between value orientation and economic condition on the other. His model in the presented paper envisages education as an agent bringing about change in economic conditions and inter-tribal differences in the Christian and Non-Christian Oraons and the Kharias.

With his vast experience in tribal field, in his keynote address Dr. S.P. Gupta, while discussing the tribal health takes the view-point of the tribals of Chotanagpur and pleads their concept of health, disease and their remedy. One soon becomes aware that the Chotanagpur tribal beliefs and practices simply do not have any relevant connections with the modern system of medicinal practice in terms of cognition. Thus there is a wide gap between these two. He draws our attention to the tribal pharmacopoeia which is a mine of information of medicinal value yet to be explored, underlying immense economic developmental possibilities. His positive suggestions at the end may prove helpful to the planners or the related professionals as well as to the tribals.

Another example of communication gap between modern medical practices and traditional tribal practices becomes apparent from the case study reported by Choudhary and Khashmisi in their study of Bhoskas of Nainital. They trace the magnitude of belief in spiritual cure of the diseases. According to them evil spirits cause diseases that is why they sought magical therapy in the cure of diseases such as jaundice, abscess, headache and dog bites with fullest satisfaction on patient's behalf. Their suggestions revolve around the attitude system. For instance, the beneficial or scientific part of their magic can be taken into consideration while practising modern medicine and secondly long term planning for community participation may be tried. In the latter the tribal folk could be educated in various medical and paramedical streams and in turn they may serve their fellow men of their area.

In his paper, Haque presents the health condition and nutritional status of Bhil and Garasia, two important tribal groups of Rajasthan, through anthropometrical parameters and indices. He concludes that they are under-nourished. The most important point which he raises is the identification of cultural value oriented constraints under an abundantly food reserved environment which may sometimes bring about malnutrition in some populations.

A.N. Sandhwar in his brief case study of Korwas presents a vivid picture of the grave health problem. He sees the whole phenomena as a vicious circle. Their health deterioration and sufferings have links with the non-availability of clean water and thereby forcing them to use stagnant, dirty water pools which are the sources of infection. Their skin gets infected and spreads more due to lack of clothes and proper washing, consequently facing social ostracism from the nearby people. It can be an example of emotional disintegration having deep roots in health, education, ecology and economy of the tribals.

While stressing the role of developmental agencies in a tribal area Dipesh Choudhury and S.K. Pal present a case study from the Juang tribes of Orissa. They were shifting cultivators but with the endeavour of non-governmental development agencies they have become settled agriculturists. These agencies acquainted them with the various agricultural implements and provided loans from banks. The other two programmes which they ran were on Education and Health improvement ones. Through proper motivation the education and literacy rate increased considerably. The medical facilities were delivered at the door step of these tribals. Regular door to door survey was made and if some one was found to be suffering was advised to contact the medical officer of the nearby government dispensary. However, to bring about a change in the sphere of social and economical aspects is quite difficult. Even more, if it deals with tribals having lesser outside contacts. Their demographic structure, socio-cultural attitudes are difficult to change. In the end from the practical field experience the authors suggest few ideas through which the problems faced by the tribals and development agencies can be solved.

The present purpose in summarily considering individual contributions to this book has been to show some of the main interlinking themes which relate to the overall understanding of the Tribal problems leading to tribal disintegration from the "Main Stream" of our National Culture. This may not be obvious at first sight, partly because it is difficult in any multiauthored book to achieve continuity of argument, but more so because in this complex field our knowledge and understanding is limited and patchy. There are more important components especially related to the Tribal economy and the ongoing developmental activities or National plans for tribal upliftment, which have not been closely considered here. We may perhaps then look forward to the day when all aspects of this problem can be seen with wholeness which now eludes us. I hope that this book will contribute something to bring that day nearer.

TWO

Tribal Development and National Integration

Justice Anand Prasad Sinha,

After 37 years of independence , to think and discuss about tribal development appears to be really strange but, however, that is a reality and it becomes extremely necessary today when a feeling of social solidarity and complete political unity has become a compelling factor in order to maintain frontiers and unity of the country intact.

There have been consistently two difficulties in real development of the tribals, one existing inside and the other outside. Because of the traditional way of life and concept of magic oriented notions, the tribals have always resisted any reformation, education and transculturisation, purely on a feeling that any such importation of thought is a challenge to their existence. The outside difficulty is that on account of peculiar way of thinking of the tribals any organisation including the State have not properly appreciated which is the right side first to tackle for the development.

So far, an attempt to unfold the historical backgrounds of the tribals, enough seems to have been done but little have been towards sociological or analytical aspect keeping in mind that tribal development really meant social, economic and cultural upliftment purely for the good of tribals importing the theme "the greatest happiness of the greatest number". Whenever, the leaders amongst the tribals have stood up, I have a feeling that the activities have been purely political, either to maintain their existence or with a sense of thrill and sensation. Hardly, there has been an attempt to work for social and economical upliftment. I have not seen the demand for free schooling of the tribals and good institutions for proper learning but agitation had been for cutting of the jungles and the like. In this vicious circle, the whole notions among the tribals which are definitely impediments towards their real development have persisted. On account of lack of education and at the same time half of education has made a tribal unfit either for agricultural operation or for any industry but they have become idle wanderers associated with crimes. The notion of witchcraft is so strong that every third murder in the tribal area amongst the tribals is on account of the fact that the deceased was suspected witch. Is it not unfortunate that after several years of independence and there being a cry of Tribal development, the State Government has not been able to properly educate and make the tribals understand that the notion of witchcraft is a myth. On the contrary, the person accused of committing murder is awarded the maximum sentence provided in law, either death or imprisonment for life. How do you expect a proper development if such impediments are in the way. There are several researches but there is no time to give illustration except to comment, that wrong notions prevailing in the minds of the tribals can only be removed if there is proper development both of mind and living conditions. In this background, any attempt of tribal development appears to be futile unless, in addition to the Government Social Organizations, Institutions, Universities and correct leadership whole-heartedly take up this matter with selfless zeal to do or die. I can assure you that the conditions of today are much better and improved. Thanks to the Anthropology Department of the Ranchi University with which I was associated for several years while posted at Ranchi as Judicial Commissioner. The problem of tribal development had been taken by them side by side, of historical exposition of the life and living of the tribals.

Coming to the problem of National Integration, in the outset, I would like to say that society is formed when two individuals enter into reciprocal relationships. One individual standing in the centre of Sahara desert or at the top of Himalayas cannot be said to have formed any society whatsoever. Today formation of the society at the initial stage of human life appears to be inevitable. If that be so, how the important bulk of the population can be totally ignored from being added in one unit which has become necessary today for the overall development of the nation. All systematic thinking about the National Integration is linked at one end with political theory. Naturally, this makes a thinking man search of making of better unification and its failure is a failure of the democracy and national strength. No Nation can afford to allow any neglect of national integration vis-a'-vis' development of the society. The society has a close link with entire population and ultimately that society growing bigger and bigger merges with the concept of Nation. The tribal development is a definite systematic growth and strength and that strengthens the strength of the people and that strength lies with Nation. The Nation loses its integrity in its absence. Therefore, this has necessitated the protection of individuals including the tribals which are part and parcel of our society and members of brotherhood.

Therefore, it is a demand of the day that both the State and the Social organizations depute selfless workers and help in the real development of the tribals so that the unity and integrity of the nation is maintained.

THREE

Education and Value System: A Key-note Address

K. N. Sahay

I

Education is an unique process which aims at an alround development of man i.e., physical, mental, moral and spiritual. Besides, man is a 'Social' and 'Culture-building' animal, and he has to adapt himself to a given geographical environment in which he lives and at the same time modify the environment according to his needs. Education is such an instrument which takes care of all these aspects related to man and helps him to turn out the best in him with a view to achieve these objectives.

Education is a broad and multi-faceted concept and the objective referred to above can be achieved in a number of ways. The education may be formal or informal; traditional, technical or non-technical. It may be related to health, sex, morality, religion, human values and artistic expressions, different occupations, human interactions, the mundane world or the spiritual world. It may be related to bookish knowledge or may be in the form of diverse experiences of life. Again, there may be various standards of formal education viz., primary, secondary, college or higher education.

II

Originally, during Vedic times education was considered as a part of 'holy process' passing from a *Guru* to *Shishya*. The *Guru* would train the mind and heart of the students to enable them to face the life with conviction and courage (Sinha, 1958).

Vedas contained both types of knowledge; *Apara* and *Para*. The *Apara* relating to worldly knowledge, was essential for success in the mundane world while the *Para* was concerned with spiritualism. The two were however not polarized. They constituted a continuum and were part of the ancient curriculum of education. In mundane world, life was always guided by the principles laid down by religion and spirituality.

Education in India today has lost its ancient spirit. Nineteenth century witnessed the advent of Marx who stressed the fruit of labour. "Intellectuals were devalued and were put on the same level as had labourers". This, combined with the expansion of *Pay Brittanica* in India among others, brought in its train materialism, scientific outlook and secularization and decried religion and spiritualism. It gradually wiped off some basic traditional and positive values inherent in the ancient system of education. Now, by and large, the teachers became more mercenary and they were least interested in enriching the mind and heart and building the character of the students concerned (Ibid).

Here, we may observe that education is upholder and perpetuator of established values as well as is itself determined by the prevailing value system of a society. Education and value system are entwined together and interdependent. At the same time it is to be noted that a new educational system may create altogether new values and serve as a harbinger of change. In ancient India during the time of *Rishis* our's had a spiritually oriented society and the *Gurukul* system of education would uphold preserve this orientation of the people. But in modern times when the Britishers introduced the western system of education, it cut us off from our spiritual moorings, as a result of which many old and positive values of *Ashrama* fell into disuse.

Of late, specially after independence we have come to realize that the British system of education suffers from certain lacuna and we are anxious to bring reform in it. As a result, we have made experiment after experiment to achieve this objective. But it seems the legacy still continues and yet another major change in the educational system is in the offing.

Here, it is important to note that modernity and spirituality - and the two sets of values associated with it, may not be always contradictory. They constitute two poles of the same continuum. If we opt for development, technological progress and material prosperity it is fine, but at no stage we should forget about the gradual culmination of material life into a spiritual life. If we could do it and if that be the condition of our material progress, we may be able to forge a new society (Sahay, 1985). What is suggested here is to accept a change within the framework of Indian ethos that will take care of both the things. The new system of education has to take this basic point into account.

In relation to tribal people it has been found that education goes a long way in dispelling many traditional values related to superstitions that serve as a great hinderance to development and progress. It partly goes to account for partial acceptance or total rejections of several Innovations beneficial to a community even though the people are logically convinced about its merits. Education makes the mind 'open' and increases the 'acceptibility' and 'appreciation' of innovations.

It has been realized that change cannot be 'imposed' on the tribals whatsoever fair our intention may be. For being of lasting importance, change must come from within. Before any meaningful change is introduced in their society, a change must be brought in their value system. And values could be changed only through effective and proper education.

IV

India is a heterogenous country with a great amount of diversity in terms of ethnic linguistic, religious and other affiliations. Due to it the Indian Constitution laid down certain principles, the spirit of which must pervade our educational system. Hence fostering the spirit of national solidarity constitutes the prime concern of our educational system as the *NATION* cannot progress unless all fissiparous tendencies are subdued and we think in terms of national integration. It is a challenging task before the educational system of the country.

Education in India has a deep colonial impact on it. The Britishers did not fail to distort even our history. (Mohiuddin, 1984). Hence what is needed is to undo the colonial influence and write a fresh history of India with a view to educate the people on a factual basis in the interest of harmony and integration among its diverse people.

One finds the element of colonialism also in the field of social sciences. The early British administrators, did not have any real understanding of the problem or some Christian missionaries considered the tribals as distinct from Hindus. But a tribe is a 'structural concept' and it would be difficult to distinguish a tribe and caste on 'cultural level'. It is high time that such misgivings which strengthen the negative forces be immediately removed.

Ethnic heterogeneity of the country and the idea of 'Unity in Diversity' also requires to have a policy of education which on the one hand upholds and perpetuates distinct cultural values of the various ethnic or regional groups, while on the other, integrates such values within the broad framework of the value system of the country as a whole. To illustrate, for the tribals of Chotanagpur, the courses should no doubt eulogize the role played by Birsa Munda, Jatra Bhagat and the like in the freedom struggle of this region, but it must be done in the state, regional and national perspectives so that the tribals not only treat them as exclusive leaders of the tribals but associate them with and place them in the ranks of many other freedom-fighters of the state, region and country. Similarly, when we talk of tribal religion or other cultural usages, it is also necessary to give them a comparative idea of non-tribal religious or corresponding cultural usages of other Indian communities. In this process, the tribes would automatically view their achievements with reference to the country and thus would be always conscious of the 'part' and 'whole' relationship.

Teaching of at least two other Indian languages from other regions of the country besides one's own mother tongue may be made at the school and college stages on compulsory basis to form an integral part of the basic course which again may have a very salutory effect and will foster a sense of unity among the various ethnic groups.

Again, it goes in the interest of the nation to have an uniform and countrywide educational curricula with some allowance for a local or regional bias specially in case of tribal areas and the like. This will create a sense of integration among the students belonging to different parts of the country and at the same time help to preserve the distinct cultural heritage of the different people. It may be accommodated by having two types of bodies, National and Regional. The National body should provide guidelines for curricular formation on the post-graduate level, while the Regional body should look after the undergraduate courses (Vidyarthi, 1985:4).

V

There cannot be two opinion that education, specially higher education, should conform to international standards and incorporate within it latest discoveries in the different fields of learning. But what is important is that simultaneously, education should be also indigenized and have an Indian bias. By and large, the present generation is made to think that scientific knowledge came from West, quite oblivious of the fact that many ancient *Rishis* and men of learning were great thinkers and inventors of scientific ideas, be it aeronautics, physics, medical, veterinary engineering sciences or astronomy.

Besides, the Hindu concept of *Dharma* and *Purusartha* developed by ancient Indian thinkers relate to the basic principles which bind the society together, foster a sense of solidarity and make an alround development of man. It upholds saner, sober elements in the society, a fact so much stressed in the writings of the structural anthropologists like Durkheim, Radcliff-Brown and others in modern times (Sahay, 1985:23).

We can very well say that higher education should have two functions i.e., firstly to create excellence in all the fields of knowledge, and secondly to maintain and enhance the civilizational traditions of India (Vidyarthi, 1985). Evidently the civilizational traditions will not only mean those traditions which are uniform on the country wide level but which also include regional and sub-regional cultural traditions including those of the tribals which are diverse but underlying elements of unity.

VI

Whenever we talk of education, our mental exercise usually relates to 'formal education' that we impart through educational institutions. Informal education has not so far received its due share of importance. But it is felt that informal education wields a greater and more profound influence on us because it is pervasive, unseen, unstructural, diffused, implicit and to some extent beyond our control. This influence may be positive or negative and we get caught unaware into it. Hence it needs a more careful planning. In a way, we are undergoing constant process of informal education even when we talk on the road, or interact with others in the given socio-cultural milieu, sit in a cinema hall, or even while we go to bed and switch on Radio or T.V.

The situation requires a two pronged approach. Firstly, we have to recognize the importance of informal education, locate its various sources, and make them planned so that it exerts a positive and systematic influence on the people as we wish. Secondly, we have to admit that we cannot exercise effective control over all the sources of informal education. Under the circumstances, all we can do is to evolve a mechanism which could neutralize the negative influence of informal education.

Cinema, Radio and Television are powerful means of communication. No doubt, there are some programmes of formal education on these media for various sections of the people with different interests but apart from that, the entertainment programmes have also the context of informal education and value orientation. Some of the Television programmes like the series on *Bibi Natiyon Wali* teach us in an effective manner the human values above religious comediettions and a deep concern for others; *Darpan* literally meaning 'mirror' and reflecting what was happening in the Indian society through the medium of best stories selected from different linguistic-cultural areas, reinforces some widely accepted moral lessions and values as well as gives practical wisdom in the changed context of society; regional films acquaint us with regional culture of India and help strengthening the spirit of national integration; *Hamlog* fosters a sense of inter-regional harmony and integration, upholds the ideal of joint family; enlightens us on some aspect of family quarrels and other things; *Paying Guest* upholds the moral of being good and helpful to others; *Rajni* exposes the evils of our society and gives us an awareness of our rights and duties and so on. Some foreign serials bring to our drawing room the way of life of the people of other country which would have been otherwise impossible and playing important role in increasing the general knowledge of the viewers, widening their horizon and moulding a healthy attitude and world view.

T.V. stations have been opened in some tribal areas as well like Chotanagpur and Madhya Pradesh and such T.V. stations can play a vital role in preserving, reinforcing or reviving the basic tribal values which are obsolete and depicting the life and adventures of their cultural heroes which give them a sense of dignity and respect for their cultural heritage, and at the same time creating such values through carefully made programmes which helps them to bring into the main stream of national life or inform the general viewers about the life and conditions of our tribals.

But at the same time such media of communication may exert some negative influence as well. Many people including children have a tendency to view all types of programmes which they do at the cost of their study or other important works. This thing has to be controlled. Some of the advertisements flashed through these media are conspicuous. What the *Lambardar Ki Bahu* confides to her friend several times on Radio is listened to by millions of children of unripe age and they are bound to discuss about it among their friends. But why should a fragment of the knowledge of sex implicit in this advertisement come to them so abruptly and systematically. A little and sporadic knowledge may be dangerous. Why not initiate a systematic and planned education for children relating to the fundamentals of sex.

Hot Track and Rock line showing western dances and music constitute one of the most favourite programmes on T.V. for many youngesters and the opinions are sharply divided over the question of desirability of such programmes. However, I personally feel that no music whatsoever alien, is bad so long they are the source of joy. Hence, there should not be any bias and restriction on it. Rather we should make the presentation of our own Indian music more attractive. One of the reasons behind the attractions and popularity of western music is that it is attractive at the 'surface' though its effect is short lived while the Indian classical music for many people is attractive at the core and is intrinsic and spiritually oriented. Just presentation of classical music is not sufficient, rather the audience have to be educated in comparative evaluations of the two systems of music. The whole mechanism of Indian music has to be laid bare before the audience to demonstrate and prove its uniqueness, spiritual context and edge over the western music, if we really want to educate our people and preserve the cultural heritage.

Another important source of informal education is family circle where children are socialized in basic norms of the society. But now in the changed context, specially ceased to fulfil this role satisfactorily. It needs to be revived or strengthened. In tribal areas the children may be socialised in tribal lores through folk tales, riddles and the like.

One may also recall the valuable contribution which youth dormitories would make in many tribal societies. Such dormitories used to have valuable economic, social, religious and cultural functions. It would serve as a nucleus of village activities and the inmates worked in the interest of the village. The inmates thus underwent valuable informal training in the tribal norms and disciplines. Unfortunately however, youth-dormitories have now virtually declined under the impact of modernity but it is felt that this institution can be very well revived with some modification and addition in its function to suit the changed needs of the society.

The tribal people have been traditionally known for many good things in their culture like truthfulness, honesty, integrity, simplicity and mutual-cooperation. But these rare traits are fastly ending under the impact of modernity. The youth-dormitories may help to revive and re-inculcate these valuable tribal attributes through informal education.

VII

With regard to formal education it may be observed that moral and spiritual education should form an integral part of the curriculum right from nursery classes upto High school standard. These courses must get a high priority value. Our great cultural and spiritual heritage and contribution of different regional and tribal communities, inter-ethnic harmony, universal truths as reflected in different religions and subjects having a bearing on inter-religious, inter-regional, inter-linguistic and national integrations which also underlie the conceptions of *Dharma* and *Purusartha* should carefully be combined and phased (Sahay, 1985).

Today it has been found that students in general do not take interest in their study. Partly it is because conventional syllabus not oriented to real life problems or which does not care to utilize the potentialities of students, has ceased to be of any interest to them. A new syllabus may be framed taking into consideration these points. Besides conventional syllabus which forms the core there may be optional courses on sports, stage-performances, trekking, mountaineering, painting, film-making, social service, technical training relating to Radio, T.V., automobile or other vocational jobs. The tribal boys and girls have already made their mark in the field of sports and earned laurels. Music, painting, trekking, mountaineering, stage performance, painting and engineering may be some other fields which may suit the genius of tribals and they are most likely to shine in these fields. What is needed is to locate the talents through proper devices and nurture them with care. A handful of such boys and girls who are extraordinary may be sent to reputed institutions of the country for training. There they may imbibe the spirit of national unity in the company of students coming from other regional and cultural background. On completion of their training, they may be sent back to their own areas where similar institutions may be opened under their guidance which should continue locating more talents and train them. There may be a country wide network of such institutions and the Government should utilise their service to meaningful ends. We would be doing a great service to the tribals if we could help them to develop a 'creative minority' among them which in due course takes care of their own people particularly in relation to CREATIVE and some other finer aspects of culture.

VIII

Lastly, education and value system, leads us to the question of 'effectiveness' of education which is vital. There are three aspects of it; education imparted, education received, and utility of education in fulfilling professed ends. Education implies communication, and communication involves words. The words must prove effective and inspire the listeners otherwise it is nothing more than a noise. Words have been equated with *Bramha* and it shows the sacred origin of it. So, to be effective, communicative and purposeful, they must be used preferably by such people who are puritans of good moral character and exemplary, in other words of a *Sattuika* temperament as far as possible.

REFERENCES

Mazumdar, D.N. 1956: An Introduction to Social Anthropology, Asia Publishing House, Lucknow.

Mohiuddin, M. 1978: Education for National Integration, The Indian Nation, Wednesday, August 15, 1984 (Supplement)p. 1-2

Sahay, K.N. 1984: The study of culture change in Tribal Bihar in 'Field Studies on the People of India: Methods and Perspective by Surajit Sinha (ed.) Indian Anthropological Society, Calcutta.

Sahay, K.N. 1985-86: "Dharma and Purusartha and Its Relevance to the situation of cultural Crisis in Modern India" in Journal of Social Research Vol. 28-29 No. Sept-March.

Sinha, B.M.K. 1985: Education in Essence, The Indian Nation, Sunday, April 28, Sunday Magazine, Page 1.

Vidyarthi, L.P. 1985: Needed Higher Education in India (MSS) Presented in a meeting sponsored by RAA and Chotanagpur Education Council at Ranchi.

FOUR

Innovation in Modern Educational System with Special Reference to Tribes of Chotanagpur

B.N. Sahay

Education plays an important role in nation building. The future of the nation depends much on the education of the forthcoming generations. This makes us realize on one hand the necessity of educating each and every citizen of the country and on the other to decide what type of education should be imparted to the coming and growing generations.

Regarding world's illiteracy, Dr. Frank C.L. Laubach reported on July 22, 1946 to UNESCO that about 60% of the world's population is still illiterate. In Asia this is 80% to 90% and in Africa it is 96%. In Europe illiteracy is practically non-existent in the following countries - Denmark, Norway, Sweden, Finland, the Netherlands, Switzerland and Germany. In England and Scotland it is only one percent. According to Indra Kumar (1951-52) in education, India holds a very poor position. Here literacy rate is only 36 percent (1981 census). Among the tribals, it is further low or in certain tribes it is approximately nil. Among nomadic Birhors of Bihar it is totally nil, among Kolha of Sambalpur, Orissa it is only about 4 percent (Sahay,1979 (i)' 84(ii). In view of national integration, it is urgently required to develop all the backward communities including tribes of the nation and bring them at least above the poverty line. In development education is very much helpful.

Keeping in view present educational system and its role in development of backward communities and national integration, this study has been framed. The paper deals with mainly merits and demerits of present educational system, scope of modification in it and the problems being faced by the students specially tribals in continuing education.

Data have been collected occasionally during past three years by discussing and interviewing individually or in groups more than 500 individuals, which includes students, teachers of schools, colleges and universities, research scholars, guardians of students and administrators of education departments. Collection of data was confined mainly to Bihar and Bengal and partially to Orissa, Assam and Meghalaya.

"If we go to the root meaning of the word "Education", we find that it is derived from the Latin word "educare" meaning "to educate", 'to bring up' 'to raise' all, as they say in America, or clever, as they say in France.

There are some other words which are cited as basic to the meaning of education. For example, the word educare which means "to lead out", or the other explanation based on the meaning of the Latin 'c' standing for 'out of' and "duco" for 'to lead'.

Thus 'education' is leading out what is within man. It is by means of education that the latent potentialities of man are made patent.

We see that in general there are two meanings given to the word 'education'. One meaning lays emphasis on the training and teaching, and the other on the "leading forth" or enabling the individual to develop according to his potentialities.

Mahatma Gandhi considered that education is worthwhile which enabled one to have 'Mukti' i.e. freedom from all vices and freedom to develop oneself materially and spiritually.

In the view of Vivekanand, the ideal of all education, and training, should be the man-making. But, instead of that, we are always trying to polish up the outside. What is the use in polishing up the outside when there is no inside? The end and aim of all training is to make the man grow. "The characteristics of the Brahmanic system of education (i.e. post-Vedic periods) was realization of the self and following the fourfold path of life's objective viz. Dharma, Artha, Kama and Moksha. Moksha, Nirvana or liberation was the highest goal and the immediate goal was living a life in accordance with the rules of caste (Varna) and stages of life (Ashram). Knowledge of this world helped the child to prepare for his future social life, and knowledge of the higher type 'Paravidya' helped him to attain the spiritual life hereafter leading to emancipation and self-realization". (Safaya 1975).

If we analyse the definition and above mentioned explanations in present context we may understand in its four folds i.e. education and social values, education and economy, education and health and education and spiritual development. Thus we may define education as the teaching and training of an individual which makes him socially a good citizen, to earn his livelihood, to lead a physically good life, and finally spiritually developed.

The result of modern educational system is not satisfactory even in its any of the above mentioned four aspects i.e. social, economic, health and spiritual field.

1) Education and social values: Present educational system has certainly played a great role in economic development of the nation. We have achieved self sufficiency in food and agriculture, did much advancement in the fields of science and technology, medicines and surgery, games and sports and even in stepping on moon-land. But simultaneously this educational system has caused much damage to the society. We have lost very-very important part of our social life i.e. social/moral values; the role of which in the social structure is like the cement in a concrete building. It helps in developing social relations between man and man and thus cause the formation of social structure. In its absence we have developed in the society a sense of insecurity, disonesty, insincerity, selfishness, disregard to elders and teachers, anti-community, anti-National feeling etc. We lack attitude and feelings of nationality, patriotism, kind heartedness and truthfulness. Today, no sphere of society seems to be free from corruption. One cannot believe the military personnel protecting the nation, the administrators who have shouldered the task of developing the poor and backwards, the businessmen who play major role in the economy of the society and even the friend in need, father and

mother in family affairs, wife and husband in their relations. This situation is not only prevailing in Indian subcontinent, but more or less the whole world is passing through this stage. Any moment the whole complex social structure of the world may collapse due to the fault committed in selfishness by any leading personality of any super power country.

So, by lacking the specific qualities of the humanity we cannot protect our society and maintain world peace. Our one sided development in material world may lead us to our destruction. Thus ourselves, the generators of modern world, as well as, the coming generation may not get chance to take its benefit in future.

Therefore, there is urgent need to bring both the physical thinking and the social values nearer to each other and in future develop the both side by side.

The development of social values in an individual, is the part of his socialization, which occurs in the family, society and educational institutions. On administrative level, it is not possible to control the social situation in the family and the society on mass basis. But we can influence it slowly by help of mass media like television, radio, newspapers and magazines by presentation of good plays, drama, story etc., based on the required social values.

Besides family and society educational institutions play a great role in formation of personality of the children. Therefore, it is advisable to introduce a course based on moral science. Several missionary schools do follow such courses and maintain discipline, that is why they produce better citizens so far discipline and moral character is concerned. Keeping the importance of discipline and moral value in views such courses may be taught compulsorily in all educational institutions upto intermediate course. Such courses may be developed on the basis of good stories available in modern and religious texts. Time to time written and oral examination of such study may be taken by the teachers of the institutions. The teachers of the educational institutions should call joint meetings of the guardians of the students and should suggest them to behave and guide the children in the family according to the social values being taught in the schools/colleges. Such type of teachings in educational institutions and suggested role played by the mass media will certainly bring some good result so far process of personality development of the new generation is concerned.

2) Education and Economy: The aims and objectives of the education are to prepare the individual economically independent so that he may earn his livelihood sufficiently and lead his life happily. But against this norm, today's education has created problem of unemployment. Most of the educated individuals do not want to labour to earn their livelihood. They have developed a tendency to get without doing any labour or sacrifice for it. Such tendency among youth is doing harm to the economy of the society.

No where in India unemployment is so acute among the illiterate as among the educated. The illiterates do not hesitate to engage themselves in commonly available work which requires physical labour. On the other hand, our educated during the course of their education have developed hesitations to do any type of physical labour. Such mentality is the root cause of their unemployment. So to eradicate unemployment problem and to make the educated youth hesitation free in doing physical labour, the students are required to undergo training in courses based on physical labour.

In preparation of such courses the regional economy may be kept in view. For example, in the school located in and around the forest area, students may be given training of work related to forest economy like preparation of furniture, collection of forest products etc. Similarly in agriculture based societies, students may be given physical training in highly developed techniques of cultivation and dairy farming. Such training will make the students hesitation free from taking up any locally available work and this will help our society in solving the present day unemployment problem.

3) Education and Health: In absence of good health one cannot enjoy his life, so one must learn to maintain a good physique. India is rich in *yoga* teachings. By *yoga* one can easily maintain a good health. Keeping this in view in each and every educational institution courses based on *yoga* may be made compulsory specially upto secondary education. For it, good *yoga* teachers may be employed. Learning of *yoga* may help the students in leading a disease free long

life. Secondly, among the unmarried youth it will help in controlling sex behaviours, which is very necessary in country like India, where sex enjoyment is prohibited for unmarrieds. Thirdly, the high expenses and complexities of allopathic system of treatment may be avoided by adopting yogic exercises for curing different diseases. This does not require high expenses of hospital also. Recently our President, Mr. Giani Zail Singh has also recommended *yoga* teachings in a public address keeping the above mentioned facts in view.

4) Education and spiritual development : The goal of the human life is to attain *moksha* (salvation) or is to get his soul mixed with upper soul or super power or self realization. So keeping the objective in view for spiritual development each and every student should be given training of meditation and concentration. In this regard student may have freedom to follow his own religion. This will develop religious harmony and national integration.

The practice of *yoga* will help the students in the field of meditation and maintaining mental peace also.

Thus following the four above mentioned aspects of education certainly our educational institutions will produce citizens suitable to our society.

REFERENCES

Abdulla, G. Rasool, 1973: The Educational Ideas of Maulana Abdul Kalam Azad, Sterling Publishers (P) Ltd. New Delhi.

Airan, J.W., 1979: College Education in India, Sachin Publications, Ajmer.

Bajwa, Ranjit, S & Wilfred R. Smith, 1980: Educational Sociology: A Modern Cultural Approach, The Indian Publications, Ambala Cantt., India.

Coombs, Philip H. (etal), 1976: New Paths to Learning, Vidya Mandal, Delhi.

Jayaswal, Sita Ram, 1972: Principles of Education, Prakashan Kendra, Aminabad, Lucknow.

Joad, C.E.M. (year not given): About Education, Faber & Faber Limited, 24 Russel Square, London.

Kothari, Education Commission (1964-66), Govt. of India, Delhi

Mukherjee, K.C., 1967: Under development Educational Policy And Planning, Asia Publishing House, New Delhi.

North, Alfred, 1954: The Aims of Education, The New American Library, New York.

Rao, T.V. (etal), 1980: Adult Education for Social Change. Manohar Publication, New Delhi.

Safaya, Raghunath, 1975: Development, Planning and Problems of Indian Education, Dhanpat Rai & Sons, Delhi.

Seetharamu, A.S., 1980: Education and Rural Development, Ashish Publishing House, New Delhi.

Sharma, O.P. (year not given), Education for National Progress, Anu Prakashan, Meerut, India.

Topo, Sita, 1979: Dynamics of Educational Development In Tribal India, Classical Publications, New Delhi.

FIVE

University Education Among the Tribals: Chotanagpur A Case Study[1]

Anil Kishore Sinha

Education is an unique process through which an individual learns about physical, mental, moral and spiritual development in all respects. It determines psycho-physical traits of a person towards a certain desired goal of life. Education also contributes to the moral and spiritual development to a certain extent.

According to the International Commission on the Development of Education set up by UNESCO, the objective of education should be to develop the complete man. Apart from this general objective, our Constitution lays down certain principles, the spirit of which must pervade our educational system. Hence one of the prime concerns of our educational process must be the fostering of the spirit of national solidarity.

"Before 1976, education was exclusively a responsibility of the States the Central Government being concerned directly with certain areas like co-ordination, determination of standards in technical and higher education etc. In 1976, by a Constitutional amendment, education became the joint responsibility of the Central and State Governments. However, the primary responsibility continues to be that of the States." (Government of India, 1983 : 47).

---

1. The present study is based on a brief fieldwork conducted by the present author among the post-Graduate tribal students of Ranchi University, Ranchi in the year 1983 under the auspices of a Research Project on "University Education and Tribal Society" conducted by Dr. V.S. Upadhyay.

Under article 46 of the Constitution, promotion of educational interest of Scheduled Tribes is a special responsibility of the Central and State Governments. The Government is, therefore, extending various facilities for the promotion of education among Scheduled Tribes.

University education in India has a long history. The Universities like Nalanda, Takshashila in India were the leading centres of learning in the contemporary world and attracted scholars from other countries. "The first University of India was started in Calcutta in January, 1857. The 9th January, 1863 is a memorable day for Bihar as the Patna College was established on that date. The establishment of the Patna University in 1917 opened a new Chapter in the history of higher education in Bihar. The earliest effort towards starting college education in Ranchi District dates back to 1927 when I.A. classes were opened in Ranchi Zila School and affiliated to Patna University." (Upadhyay, 1983 :76).

"Considering the urge and demand of the tribal population, the Government of Bihar created the University of Ranchi by an Act of Legislature on 12th July, 1960. The idea behind creating a new University in Chotanagpur, which is mainly inhabited by tribal population, was to give certain special facilities for the admission of tribal students into various colleges. It has its jurisdiction over all the affiliated colleges, located in the districts of Ranchi, Hazaribagh, Dhanbad, Palamau and Singhbhum." (Toppo, 1979 : 211). "By the end of 1983 there were 40 Constituent colleges and 36 affiliated colleges of Arts, Science and Commerce under Ranchi University" (Christodoulou, 1984 : 1786 - 1802). Besides there are two Medical Colleges, one Law College, one Teacher's Training College, two Engineering colleges and one Diploma in Mental Disease course attached to Kanke Mental Hospital.

The University education has to meet the increasing demand for every type of education such as literary, scientific, technical and professional. By the application and development of technical and scientific knowledge, the country will attain freedom from economic wants, diseases and ignorance. University education is meaningful and beneficial to the individual and society as it automatically leads to gainful employment opportunities and makes one intellectually broader. In the context of tribal people, the University education should also take its due place.

How University Education is Different From Other Education?

University education is different from other types of education as it is meant for only those who have a requisite standard and aptitude for scholastic attainments. But at the same time one cannot totally ignore the fact that the number of persons engaged in University education should also be steadily increased in order to man the different specialised fields of training, education as well as management and administration. (Banerjee, 1984).

Some tribal people believe that the main purpose of University education is to provide white - collar jobs as soon as some sort of degrees are obtained and that too not to a few but to each and all. But, in real sense University education is different from training for a job. It is a hall mark of knowledge and dignity. University education is the training, development and discipline of the real man. It is education in human values, revitalising the moral and ethical approach to life.

Aims and objectives of University Education

The ideal of University Education is Wisdom along with knowledge. Education is both a training of mind and training of souls; it gives both knowledge and wisdom. Some major aims and objectives of University education are as follows :

One of the Central aims of University education is the training for leadership in the professions and in public life. It must enable youngmen and women to read with insight the record of human experience, to know the nature and consequences of ethical values, to sense the meaning of the social forces operating in the world today and comprehend the complexities and intricacies of life in all its immensity - physical, social and spiritual.

Vidyarthi (1985 :1) mentioned that "In a country like India, higher education has two functions : one to maintain and enhance the civilizational tradition of India, and two; to create excellence in all fields of knowledge."

The major task of University education is the improvement of character for national integration particularly when we try to go to the root of the problem and plan on a long range basis. A proper education with well-thoughtout strategies can bring about miracles in the field of national integration because it has the potentiality to strike at the root of the problem.

It is very clear that firstly the study of mental-life are psychological part to educate a person and secondly, physical education is the back-bone of the academic success. In the academic world, the goal of education cannot be completed, without retaining the knowledge of mental structure and its functions. So every student should have sound knowledge of mental elements and its complex functions. Similarly, physical education is an integral part of the education in general. Mostly man's life depends on sound and solid physique. For a good health physical exercise is essential. It increases and develops the power of thinking. Therefore, such type of education also comes within University education.

Educational background of the tribals

Many tribal communities have a traditional institution, the purpose of which has always been to enable the tribal men to learn the norms, values and intricacies of behaviour of their own society, and to equip them for their role in the community life. It is achieved through the institution of youth dormitory like *Dhumkuria* among the Oraons, *Giti-Ora* among the Munda and Ho.

However, such youth dormitories have fastly declined in modern times. But these may be revived to fulfil educational needs of the tribals.

The tribal people in Chotanagpur region are educationally backward. During British time, the University education was available only for the elites and the tribal people could not think of this education. After independence, this outlook changed and the government became more and more interested in the education of weaker sections of the people including the tribals under comprehensive rehabilitation programmes.

The vital statistics given below are based on a sample study of 200 tribal students of different faculties of Post-Graduate Departments under the Ranchi University. It was found that 63.5% belong to the faculty of Arts (including Commerce), 10.5% Science, 1% to Agriculture and Law, 13% to Technical and 11.5% to Education including B.Ed. and M.Ed. This shows that most of the tribal students are interested in Arts subjects. The percentage of students in the faculty of Agriculture and Education is negligible i.e. 1 %.

Regarding the capability of students in understanding the lecture and medium of instruction, the percentage of the students who do not follow it, is high (41.5%) in Arts faculty which is followed by Technical students (15%). 50% of the Science students cannot note-down relevant facts of the lectures. Although this difficulty is also faced by the Arts students, but their percentage is comparatively less, 50% Technical students faced the difficulties in practical classes, while 30% students of science faculty face this difficulty.

Again 50% students of the Arts and Technical faculties have economic problems, while this percentage is higher (60%) in Science faculty. More than 55% students of Science and Technical faculty face the difficulties in getting or locating the proper book. This percentage is very high (91%) in Arts faculty. After discussion with several lecturers it was found that the tribal students take their admission only to get scholarship and after receiving it, they did not show their interest in attending classes.

Due to such difficulties most of the students suffered a great loss of career and lost their avenues for prosperity. In most cases after matriculation examination, they enter into the college with taking the same combination, which they had taken at school level. When they appear at the examination they fail. After that, they come to the village and sit idle for two or three years. After that they try to enter into training institute with the hope that after completion of the training, they would get the job in industries. The university education in Chotanagpur has to content with this half-hearted approach of the tribal students.

Aims of University Education among Tribals

The University Education among tribals is introduced to fulfill the following objects:

i) To remove isolation of the people to some extent so that they could come forward to utilize the fruits of welfare programmes as well as education as granted to the people of India in general.

ii) To enable the tribal people to utilise the constitutional safeguards provided to them to fight against the evils and injustices, which are prevalent in the society.

iii) To remove the complex problem of inequality and inferiority, to some extent in tribal community.

iv) To bring and stimulate political mobility among the tribal community and to make the people politically conscious and to care for the rights and responsibilities towards community and nation.

v) To provide good jobs, bringing prosperity, leading to higher standard of living.

vi) To produce persons to have a say in politics, economics, education and administration.

Whether the aims are fulfilled ?

However, as we look to the present position of Tribal Education in Chotanagpur it seems to be in a bad shape and not much progress has been made in regard to the fulfilment of the aims behind University education among the tribals.

The factors given below play an important role in nullifying the aims of University education. They are as follows (Upadhyay, 1983:).

i) Mushroom growth of sub-standard colleges in recent years has diluted the academic standard.

ii) There is lack of institutions of University education in interior tribal areas.

iii) There is lack of hostel facilities for tribal students.

iv) The present curriculum of University education is defective for tribal students as it has no relevance to the life of the tribal community.

v) There is lack of guidance and counselling in the institutions of University education and there is no such agency for helping the tribal students for choosing the disciplines and providing information for the scope of the subjects in different jobs and other employment avenues made for them.

vi) There is sufficient provision of reservation in different category of jobs in promotion and other relexations and concessions to the tribal people, so that many of the students give up their education as soon get any job.

vii) There is sufficient provision of reservation in different category of jobs in promotion and other relaxations. Due to increase in enrolment of the number of tribal students in University education, there is educated unemployment, even among the tribals.

viii) There is to some extent language problem for tribal students in University education as discussed.

ix) The clock of University's examination and its academic sessions have been put behind by more than a year. Though this cancer of dislocation of examination schedules is eating into the vitals of the University for over a decade but for the last five years it has crossed all the limits.

x) The Science and Technology got progress rapidly, but as this progress is not combined with the progress of mind and spirit so it also hinders the fulfilment of the aims of University education.

There are some specific impediments in the University education felt by the tribal students which are mentioned below and which also act as barriers in the way of expansion of University education viz., illiterate background, economic backwardness, no enthusiasm on the part of students for getting better and better education, taking university education just as a part time, prejudiced outlook of tribal people, defective system of re-imbursement of stipends to the tribal students.

Conspicuous Tribal Problems

University education is passing through a phase of serious crisis. The entire educational field, right from primary to University stage is dotted with chaos, confusion and uncertainty. Education has become nobody's concern. There is a general feeling that the system and contents of University education is not satisfactory and even alarming in some ways (University Reporter, 1985). This system is not catering to the needs of tribal people in particular and others in general. Apart from general problems, the tribal students have additional problem which they face every day in University education.

Due to varied cultures and languages, the language problem has become so vulnerable that sometimes it is very difficult to maintain social and national integration in the country. At the school stage they follow regional language as the medium of instruction. But as they enter into University education suddenly the medium of instruction is changed from regional language to Hindi or English. Due to this, many tribal students have to face a lot of problems. Here the question arises as to which language should be adopted as medium of instruction in University education? Out of 200 tribal students 62.5% students want their medium of instruction as Hindi, 26% as English and only 11% as tribal language. If Hindi is used as the medium of instruction, then the problem is of availability of good books in University education especially in technical and professional education. If the tribal languages are used as medium of instruction, the problem becomes acute as there is no common tribal language which is used in one area even and which is developed enough to work as the medium of instruction in University education.

It is often said that generally the books available in either Hindi or Regional language in the market for the courses of study in Post-Graduate levels are not good and have low standard of materials of the subject.

The number of tribal students in University education is rising. The institutions have also increased. But by looking the pitiable condition of educated unemployment,[2] the tribal people are also doubting the benefits of this education. Even some people have stopped sending their wards to University education.

Due to poor ratio between the teacher and students, the tribal students usually find it difficult to contact the teachers and solve their educational problems.[3]

The University education also suffers from the problem of drop-outs to the maximum extent. The main reasons of drop-outs are cultural resistance, present system of attendance records and examination, lack of encouragements, economic backwardness and the like. A student is required to attend classes in all subjects at one time and also to appear in all the papers at one time. In some faculties there is a compartmental system but that is applicable after the candidate has appeared in all the papers of his examination at one time. In these circumstances the chances of drop-outs are comparatively more.

The Government of India and the provincial Government have reserved some percentage for the tribal youths in different categories of services. Owing to it as soon a tribal is in financial distress, at the behest of his family members he joins a service on economic grounds. This also contributes to drop-out in University

---

2. There are one crore ten lakh educated unemployed youths in the country. Among them, twenty lakh are graduates and those who have higher education, thirty lakh higher secondary and sixty lakh matriculates (The Indian Nation, dated December 9, 1984).

3. In Ranchi University, the average number of seats for students in the departments of Anthropology, Bengali, English, Geography, Geology, Psychology, Sanskrit and Urdu are 39 and the ratio between teacher and students is 1 : 6. In the departments of Economics, Hindi, History, Regional Language and Political Science the average number of seats is 144. The ratio between teacher and students in the above subject is 1:15. The average number of seats for students in faculty of Science is 27. The ratio between teacher and students in these faculties is 1:3. The ratio between teacher and students in Commerce department is 1:11.

education.

Points for Suggestions

The detailed discussions and explanations in the preceeding pages point out that the tribal societies, as in case of other development measures do need a special treatment in University education. Some of the important suggestions may be given as follows:

The institutions of University learning should be opened at those places only where the tribals are in genuine need of it. The present system of opening institutions in a haphazard manner and with such an ugly competition should be stopped.

The present curriculum of University education needs some modifications. There should be more scope for practical activities, related to the life of tribal community and work experience, must be introduced at all the levels of University education. There should be emphasis on extracurricular activities in the institutions to utilise the talents and energies of the tribal students and proper development of their personality.

"The educational curricula must be revamped thoroughly. They need to be done on two levels, national and regional. The national body should provide guidelines for curricular formation on the post-graduate level. Their implementation should be judged either by a national or regional body. On the undergraduate level, the curriculum guidelines should be provided by a regional body but their implementation may be left in the hands of appropriate state level-organisations". (Vidyarthi, 1985 :4).

There should be a clearcut policy for enrolment in University education specially technical, professional and science education so that in future there should be a scope of employment among educated tribal youths.

The question of improving the quality of University education is also inseparably linked with the question of providing better facilities to teachers in centres of University education. Unless teachers are mentally satisfied with the emoluments and facilities they get, they are not likely to put in their best.

Every institution of University education should have one guidance and counselling centre under a teacher who has aptitude for this programme.

The ratio of teacher and students should be reduced to 1 : 5 and for that more qualified teachers need to be appointed. There should be rigorous implementation of tutorial system as in the Universities of Oxford and Cambridge. Compulsory attendance at tutorials should be a must. Seminars should be organised at regular intervals and each student should participate in it. There should be internal assessment and evaluation of the performance of students at these tutorials and seminars and a grading system to be adopted at periodical tests should finally be considered.

The Vice-Chancellor should hold monthly meeting and obtain a monthly work report from all teachers to find out if they have been doing their job sincerely. There should be a rotational system of Headship, and the senior-most teacher in the University should be made the Vice-Chancellor for a period of three years.

Regarding the medium of instruction to be followed in University education, Hindi or Regional language should be adopted. But there should be the provision of English medium if it is desired by the tribal students.

Regarding the attendance and present system of examination we should follow U.S.A. higher educational system and the Semester system with 'Credits' and 'Grades.' The students who cannot complete their courses and examination requirements in the prescribed minimum time for one reason or the other, get more time if they so wish.

To make education as a powerful instrument for social, economic and cultural transformations the following steps should be taken. Firstly, education should be related to the areas of production in which tribals are engaged. Secondly, it should be linked with the requirements and aspirations of the tribals. Thirdly, it should strive to build character of cultivating social, moral and spiritual values.

Fourthly, it should hasten slowly the process of modernisation for the benefit of the tribal people and make the group more prosperous and strong. And last but not the least, it should make endeavours to bring the tribal students out of the isolated and segregated community to participate in the main stream of the country.

REFERENCES

Banerjee, Bireshwar, 1984; Quality Vs Quantity in Higher Education, The Indian Nation, dated June 3, 1984, Patna.

Christodoulou, A. 1984: Commonwealth University Year Book: 1984 (ed.), The Association of Commonwealth University, London.

Government of India, 1983: India A Reference Annual 1983 (ed.), Publication Division, Ministry of Information and Broadcasting, Government of India, Patiala House, New Delhi.

Kautilya 1984: Dangerous problem of the educated unemployed, The Indian Nation, dated December 9, 1984, Patna.

Toppo, Sits 1979: Dynamics of Educational Development in Tribal India, Classical Publication, New-Delhi.

University Reporter; 1985: Education in Bihar nobody's concern, The Indian Nation, dated May 27, 1985, Patna.

Upadhyay, V. S. 1983: University Education and Tribal Society, Project Report (Unpublished), sponsored by Ministry of Home Affairs, Govt. of India, New-Delhi.

Vidyarthi, L. P. 1985: Needed Higher Education in India, (Mimiographed) presented at the Seminar on 'New Education System' on September 14, 1985, Ranchi.

SIX

Tribal Development and National Integration Through Audio-Visual Media: The Role Performed and a Possibility

Sushil Arora

Introduction

By the term audio-visual media, I mean about those visual media of communication which when projected on screen through some technical device, gets the shape of moving and speaking images or in other words, I mean about those media of communication which are concerned simultaneously with seeing and hearing e.g. Cinema, Television and Videos.

The audio-visual media in general have its prime role in the field of communication, where the potentiality of the medium is being exploited by Governmental and non-governmental agencies e.g. the Indian Television or 'Doordarshan' as it is said in Hindi. It is being controlled by the Central Government and State Government whereas the Indian Film Industry is mostly dominated by private enterprises.

The present article is of a very general nature and the author in course of his discussion, will undertake three potent audio-visual media i.e. Cinema, television, and video and with the help of these aims to highlight on two different but correlated aspects viz first, what is being done for Tribal Development and National Integration through these media and Second, what possibly can be achieved through these media.

Cinema, Television and Video

Amongst the three audio-visual media referred to above, films or cinema is undoubtedly the most powerful media of communication,[1] which got its inception a little over eighty years ago but still it is an unparallel medium. Films are viewed by all age and sex groups though the younger generation have a special craze for it. People from different walks of life or from different sections of society viz. illiterate, literate and elite come together under one common roof and enjoy film viewing, which since its inception have remained unaffected inspite of financial and other problems attached with film viewing.

Besides its role in the field of communication the films bear relevance to society because of: (a) its capacity to entertain its audience; (b) its capacity to portray style of life, aspiration and problems of certain cross sections of society and to make people cautious about the changing concepts and values of our society; (c) its capacity to influence a section of society either because of a "sense of identity" with the characters portrayed in films or its being a "collective fantasy" for the masses. Besides, its influence has spilled to other media e.g., Radio, Television, Advertisement and Magazines.[2]

Television, still another potent and popular media like that of cinema, started since 1959 at Delhi, when it had a total coverage area of 65 kilometres only. Later on television centres were established at different places like Bombay, Srinagar, Amritsar (1973), Pune (1973), Hyderabad (1974), Cuttack (1974), Calcutta (1975), Madras (1975), Lucknow (1975), Mussoorie (1977), Kanpur (1978)

---

1. ".... more than 700 feature films are made in almost a dozen languages every year. These are watched in about 10,000 theatres by an average of 12.5 million people everyday and are exported to about 100 countries. It is the sixth largest industry employing over two million people. Its annual box-office receipts are in the region of 550 million dollars...." (Raghunath Raina, 1983:3).

2. Films "influence has spilled to other media; film-music is broadcast twelve hours a day over eighty five radio stations. Seven television centres show atleast one film and two film based programmes a week; advertisement and fashion draw upon it and over six hundred fan magazines based on the lives and loves of stars..... "(Raghunath Raina, 1983:4).

and Jullander (1979).

However, the real expansion of television centres started during the Sixth Five Year Plan. By April, 1980 there were a total number of 19 television centres out of which 7 centres (Delhi, Bombay, Calcutta, Madras, Srinagar, Lucknow) had all necessary facilities regarding telecast of television programmes, while 4 of them (Amritsar, Pune, Mussoorie and Kanpur) had only telecast centres and 8 of them Ahemdabad, Jaipur, Raipur, Hyderabad, Sambalpur, Cuttack and Gulbarg) functioning under CIET programme. Around 25% of population would witness the programmes telecast by television centres. During this plan period fully equipped television centres with a capacity of 10 KW were established at Mussoorie, Barnari, Murshidabad, Cuttack, Kodaikanal, Panjim and Vijaywada. Besides, television studios were built at Jaipur and Hyderabad. Among the other programmes there were provisions for building permanent studios at Lucknow and Calcutta, establishment of two transmission centres with a capacity of 10 KW capacity and a transmission building in Delhi. Progress has already been done under this programme while some of them are in the final phase.

Amongst the other achievements, mention may be made of: (a) approval to use INSAT for television in July 1981; (b) establishment of television centres of the capacity of 10 KW with limited production capacity at Ranchi, Rajkot, Gorakhpur, Nagpur, (c) establishment of transmission centres with lower capacity at 20 places like Jammu, Dewaria, Suratgarh, Gauhati, Ittanagar, Gangtok, Shillong, Kohima, Imphal, Agartalla, Maldah, Patna, Bhuvaneshwar, Port-Blair, Konki-Nadi, Trivandrum, Indore, Bhopal and Simla. These centres started from November, 1982 and relayed Asian Games which were held at Delhi.

The Central Government since July 1983 had prepared a special plan for the expansion of television transmission centres at the cost of 68 crores of rupees. Its objective was to bring 70% of the Indian population under television network during the Sixth Five Year Plan Period. Much has been done on war footing and the country now has a total number of 181 television transmission centres.

In this way it seems evident that upto the year 1980 the expansion of television was very slow and the programmes were available only within limited areas but as a result of the new policy of the Government in last few years, television has now a countrywide network and according to one estimate by March 1985, nearly 85% of the people were in a position to view the television programmes. This further led to the mushroom growth of the shops selling television sets.[3] The Government intends to extend it further in course of Seventh Five Year Plan Period.[4]

Video, still another potent audio-visual media, is a recent technical innovation in comparison to cinema and television. Since last few years videos are becoming popular in India not because of its expansion by Government but because of much noisy atmosphere created especially by film makers against "Video piracy", which to some extent has damaged the existing Indian Film Industry.

In view of the facts highlighted above it is evident that cinema, television and videos are the three potent and powerful audio-visual media and the Government seems to be cautious especially for the spread of television and intends to make it available even to the people living in remotest part of the country. It would now be in the fitness of things to judge as to how far the Government is capable to exploit the potentiality of these audio-visual media for Tribal Development and National Integration and what possibly can be achieved through these.

---

3. According to one estimate by 1968 there were 20,000 television sets working in the country. By 1969 - 74 four television companies had started the production of television. Presently, there are nearly 30 companies engaged in production of television sets, out of which 10 are actively engaged and there are 12 companies which operate on the country wide level. There was an increase in the television sets from 1981 onwards. In 1982 nearly four lac fifty thousand television licences were issued and according to some opinion there were nearly 25% television sets without licences and as such it may be summarized that nearly five lac sixty thousand of television sets were sold in the year 1982. (Bisaria Yugshree, September 2, 1984:8).

4. In the Seventh Five Year Plan period "out of total projected outlay of Rs.2809.67 Crores for the Seventh Plan, the Information and Broadcasting Ministry has proposed as much as Rs. 1243.87 Crores for television as against only Rs. 85.73 Crores for the film-medium (Karanjia, Screen, February 8, 1985).

Tribal Development and Audio-Visual Media

It is a fact that the audio-visual aids programme is one with which the Government of India intends to achieve the goal of tribal development. So far the exploitation of film medium for tribal development is concerned it seems that only meagre attempts have been made in this connection though the medium is capable of bringing positive results. It is evident that under a provision, feature films for the entertainment of tribals and others, are exhibited in the areas concerned but only at non-frequent intervals. This is being done at the Block level where other welfare activities for tribals and others are also being undertaken.

The Public Relations Department (PRD) of the Government of India has a separate wing entitled Film Producing Centre, which with its head offices at State level, is active in the field of production, distribution and exhibition of films along with the control and organization of photographic section. The film producing centre of PRD prepare films mainly related to (a) the welfare works being undertaken by the Government under 20 Point programme (b)production of news-reel and documentaries. These films are exhibited in Cinema Houses and in the interior places very often. When the department organises exhibitions at the interior places e.g., in Bihar, during the year 1984-85, a total sum of Rs. 7,38,400 was alloted to film producing centre and out of this amount a sum of Rs. 7,25,300 was spent by the centre and the results achieved were (a) production of Bihar Newsreel (No.30 to 36) which portrayed different works being undertaken by Bihar Government under 20 Point Programme and (b) production of nine newsreel and five documentaries of 14,000 feet approximately. It would not be irrelevant here to say that such films even though exhibited at interior places, are not exclusively meant for tribal development but indirectly it may fulfil the function of (a) making the tribals and others aware as to what is being done for their welfare by the Government and thus indirectly may provoke a few tribals to approach blocks seeking some sort of developmental aids (b) Newsreel and documentaries may extend their horizon of knowledge.

Now, so far as television and tribal development is concerned it is evident that with the expansion of television network in the country, television has turned to be "a family member" for the well-off families, whether they be tribal or non-tribal of cities, towns or villages and they are being benefitted alike. Besides usual television programmes, which are of entertainment and educative value, there are certain programmes prepared by regional television centres which are usually meant for the benefit of tribal and other farmers e.g. programmes related with agriculture, which improve their knowledge for production of certain items as well as what particular precautionary measures they should take for better production or how to save their agricultural field from parasites or how to make their method more scientific. Besides, tribal dance and drama performed by tribal and non-tribal or the drama based on the life of some eminent tribal leader creates a "sense of identity" and indirectly a pride for their culture and historical background which is losing its existence from the mental planes of the tribal living in cities and towns. The tribal dances portrayed on the event of independence of the country does a similar work in this regard.

Here it would not be out of context to mention the current policy of Central Government which, with the help of State Governments, is doing some work for expansion of "Community Television Sets" in the remotest villages and is aimed primarily for the benefit of the tribals and others especially those belonging to a much lower economic strata. In this connection some work has already been done in and around the adjacent villages of Delhi, Haryana and Uttar Pradesh. As per the figures available, the Government till now had provided 349 community Television sets in different villages of India. The Scheme is yet to be implemented in different other villages of the country e.g. in Bihar there is a provision for 700 community television sets for an equal number of villages. As per the current news obtained through Public Relations Department (Bihar), the department has obtained these television sets, the villages have already been selected but the scheme is yet to be implemented at different villages falling under Ranchi, Singhbhum Palamau, Gumla and Lohardaga districts of Bihar. These community television sets are to be established at different schools of the selected villages. This is being done so that even the ordinary people of interior places may get the benefit of different programmes being relayed by 'Doordarshan'. The entire planning for purchase, distribution and maintenance of these television sets is to be shared by the State Government in collaboration with the Education Department.

National Integration and Audio-Visual Media

Coming to the issue of National Integration, if we leave aside the concept of tribal development for a few moments and consider national integration as a separate entity, we find that among different audio-visual media, cinema undoubtedly has contributed in the field of national integration. Such contribution of cinema gets reflected first, on the organisational level which presents an ideal model of national unity and integration and second, the impact which the Indian Cinema wields through its various films. The contribution made by cinema in this regard may cover pages but considering time and space problem the author would highlight only relevant points without much emphasis on details.

On the organisational level we find that since its inception Indian Motion Picture Industry was never organised on community language or region wise in any department and at any level of responsibility. The movies are in fact an art form and economic enterprise which requires every single community and language group to participate. The filmdom itself is an example of secularism and inter-regional cordiality. It is especially so in Bombay, the centre of Hindi film production. "The artists, technicians, writers and producers come here from all parts of India. They profess every kind of religion. But in the pursuit of their common goal, that of working for and making successful films, they join hands and work as a team, often the credit titles of film feature names that suggest origins from various region and religions". (Hameedudin Mehboob, Screen, January 25, 1985:12). Besides, the cinema houses have served as a "common pool" where people from different sections of society and from different economic strata come together and enjoy film viewing.

During the times of many national crisis like wars, floods, cyclone and the like 'the Indian film-makers have reinforced India's "special unity" and preserved our traditions, consciously designed to militate against all attempts to divide the Indian humanity on grounds of creed, caste and language'. On such occasions it is also noted that "stars" of Indian cinema come together along with others of the industry and plead to the commoners for help and are positively responded. Such cases are evident, to cite a few examples, during the floods which ravaged Assam in 1950's, Andhra cyclone of 1971, wars of 1962, 1965 and 1971.

Now coming to the second part of cinema's unifying and integrating influence through films, we find that members of the film fraternity through their stories, songs and films over the years made a significant contribution towards national integration. Here we may mention films from Bombay like "Padosi", "Dharti Ke Lal", "Munna", "Dhool Ka Phool", "Mera Naam Joker" and above all films like "Saat Hindustani" and "Haqeeqat". These films either in their thematic essence or with the aid of songs pleaded for the feeling of oneness amongst the people of country. Similar is the case with films from other regions of India e.g. "Veer Pandye Kattaboman" from South India and "Pahela Aadmi" from Calcutta.

Besides, the recent victory of Amitabh Bacchan, Sunil Dutt, and Vijayantimala in Lok Sabha elections and prior to that the illness of Amitabh Bacchan and prayers for his life throughout the country makes it evident that the feeling of oneness is prevalent among us.

Now, so far as the television and national integration is concerned, it seems that some of the television programmes create feeling like "We" or "Ours" rather than "I" and "You". Amongst such programmes mention may be made of entertainment programmes like 'Humlog', those related with the life of our past or present national leaders, or those connected with independence, or those based on Army of the country or those highlighting different ecological settings of the country. The relay of these programmes and millions of people watching these are subjected to bring people under a feeling of oneness.

What Possibly Can Be Achieved?

It is evident that films and television to some extent are being exploited for tribal development and national integration though the potentiality of the medium presents before us a ray of hope that these audio-visual media may better be exhibited for more fruitful results concerning tribal development and national integration e.g. first, in providing informal education to the tribals; second, awareness among the tribals may be brought especially in certain areas connected with their life and where the Government is willing to help them e.g. publishing the welfare activities being implemented for them; Third, for minimizing the communication gaps between the tribals and the non-tribals or between the tribals and the executing machinery. Here films may be of great help. Besides, separate ethnographic video films prepared on the life and culture of different tribals, if shown to the executing machinery prior to the framing or certain planning, may help them in a better way to think of planning and execution of certain programmes i.e., what ought to be done at priority basis or what are those areas of development where they need much caution e.g., the areas connected with amalgamation of traditional and modern values. Preservation and screening of such films before the executing machinery should be made compulsory. Moreover, such films if relayed through television network highlighting the glory of tribal life and culture may serve a two fold purpose i.e. first, it will provide a "sense of identity" to the tribals and a pride for their cultural and historical background and secondly, such films viewed by the non-tribals would wash away certain misunderstanding from their mental plane leading to behavioural change for tribals. It would thus narrow down the communication gaps between the tribals and the non-tribals. Such and many other areas may well be traced where audio-visual media may perform some role. It is pleasing that Government through "community television scheme" intends an overall development of tribals and other such peoples but much will depend on the nature of programmes reaching before the tribals, foresightedness of Regional telecast centre along with that of Central for selecting programmes as per the current needs of the tribals as well as others of the country and a cautious attempt in this regard, in real sense, may only bring about positive results concerning tribal development and national integration.

REFERENCES

Bisaria, S.K., 1984: Twenty five years of Television Broadcasting ("Television Prasaran Ke Pacchis Varsh"), Article Published in a bi-monthly Hindi Magazine, YUGSHREE, September (Second) Issue No. 55, 55 Badalal Street, Upper Bazar Ranchi-834001. Edited by : Vedprakash Agrawal.

Karanjia, B.K., 1985: Film and T.V. in the Seventh Plan, Article published in

SCREEN -A Film Weekly of India, February 8:1, Edited by: B.K. Karanjia, Indian Express Newspapers (Bombay) Pvt. Ltd.

Raina Raghunath, 1983: The Contest: A Socio-Cultural Anatomy, Article published in Indian Cinema Superbazar, Edited volume by: Aruna Vasudeva & Phillippe Lenglet, 1983: 3-4, Vikas Publishing House Pvt. Ltd., New Delhi-110002.

SEVEN

Role of Education and Value System in Economic Development of Tribals: A Case Study of Oraon and Kharia Tribes of Chotanagpur

L.N. Bhagat

The issue of tribal development, an old one for discussion among the intellectuals, has recently emerged with a new interest and emphasis after the emergence of Mr. Rajiv Gandhi as the Prime Minister of India. The first ever political direction was provided by Jawaharlal Nehru, just after independence, for the upliftment of the tribals and their integration with rest of the country. He wanted us to follow what may be called "development through preservation" without in any way destroying the essentials of the rich tribal cultures which were sought to further beautify the total cultural mosaic of India. Since then the Government of India has been planning and implementing various schemes and programmes for the development of the tribal people of India. Integrated Tribal Development Project is one of the major efforts in this direction. There is a provision of sub-plan in the state plans. Tribal people are being given special consideration in the selection of beneficiaries under the Integrated Rural Development Programme. Despite these numerous efforts for the development of tribal people in tribal areas by the Government, we find very unsatisfactory result. One of the obvious reasons for this may be the ignorance or little information about the developmental programmes by the tribals owing to illiteracy or very low educational status. Tribals are generally accused of leading a traditional way of life. They may not be very responsive to the developmental programmes owing to their traditional value system. It is also very likely that the tribals, despite their desire, may not get adequate opportunity for responding to these programmes owing to the lack of necessary infrastructural facilities. These are some of the questions that automatically arise whenever we talk for the development of tribal areas.

The present paper attempts to quantify some of the basic characteristics of the tribals particularly the educational status and value system and to examine their role in determining the economic conditions of the tribal people in the case of Oraon and Kharia tribes of Chotanagpur. Such studies may be of great help to the planners at the lower level in identifying some of the constraints on the way of their development so that suitable prescriptions could be made for improving the economic conditions of the tribals through appropriate package of programmes.

Chotanagpur plateau is one of the three natural regions of Bihar with characteristics distinguishing it from the rest of Bihar.[1] The region is characterised by hilly and uneven territory and very high concentration of tribal population. The tribal concentration in the Chotanagpur region is borne out by the fact that about 92.3 percent of all tribals of Bihar reside in this region as per 1971 census. This is why the region is also called "Tribal Bihar". The Chotanagpur region of Bihar consists of the old districts of Ranchi, Hazaribagh, Palamau, Dhanbad, Singhbhum and Santhal Parganas. Oraon, Kharia, Munda, Ho and Santhal are the major tribes settled in the region. These five major tribes together cover about 83.0 percent of the total tribal population in Bihar as per the 1961 census.

It is pertinent to note here that the tribals of Chotanagpur differ from other Indian tribes in many respects such as: (a) Most of the tribals of Chotanagpur are settled agriculturists and possess land (Bhagat, 1983.a), (b) The tribal farming system is almost the same as that of the non-tribals in the region (Bhagat, 1981). Though living amid hills and forests the tribals of Chotanagpur prefer to live in villages and do not practice shifting cultivation except for a few minor tribal communities like Hill Kharia and Souria Paharia (Vidyarthi, 1964). (c) The system of communal ownership of land among the tribals, except among the Ho tribe, is also not found in Chotanagpur

---

1. See for details, Bhagat (1983.b).

but observed in other states (Goswami & Saikia, 1970 and Roy Burman & Sharma, 1970). (d) Tribal integration with non-tribals is one of the important characteristics of the Chotanagpur tribals (Sachidananda, 1964). (e) Rapid social change has been observed in the case of Chotanagpur tribals as compared to the tribals of other regions in the country.[2]

Material and Method

The study is based on the primary data collected from a tribal village "Kutua". The following considerations prevailed while selecting the village for the study: (a) It must be selecting purposely to reflect the relevant facts, (b) It must be of moderate size and away from the urban town and (c) The village should represent indigenous population of both tribal and non-tribal, preferably representing the district proportion.

Kutua is a village of newly created Gumla district (earlier it was under Ranchi district). It is about 125 Kms away from the Ranchi town and about 22 Kms in the eastern direction from Gumla. The village lies within the Gumla Macro Area where Integrated Tribal Development Project was launched in 1977. The village has a population of 1043 persons at present of which 61.3 percent are tribals. Oraon and Kharia are the major tribes residing in the village constituting 87.16 percent of the total tribals in the village. Out of 117 tribal families the number of families belonging to the Oraon and Kharia tribe are 74 and 27 respectively (see Appendix). The main occupation of the tribals in the village is cultivation, growing mainly the food crops. Tribals in the village have recently started growing groundnut as one of the cash crops. It should be noted that about 33.8 percent of the family belonging to the Oraon tribe are Christians whereas only family belonging to the Kharia tribe has opted for Christianity.

All 101 households belonging to the Oraon (74) and Kharia (27) tribes in the village were interviewed personally and their answers

---

2. Studies indicating social change among the tribals of Chotanagpur are Bougaert (1975), Ivern (1969), Lal (1963), Prasad (1961), Sen (1968), Sinha (1982) and Vidyarthi (1971).

noted in the Schedule prepared for the purpose. The interview was made during the month of October 1984. Thus the data used in this study are the results of classification and tabulation of the primary information collected from the head of the households through the personal interview method.

On the basis of the information collected from 101 households we have computed the educational scores and value-orientation scores and estimated the total annual income of the households. The following methods have been employed while computing the scores.

Educational Score: In preparing the educational scores of the households we have included both formal schooling and informal learning. Contact with the Extension Officers particularly VLW, listening to the transistor, visiting the urban town, and engagement in hand pounding of paddy and trading rice in the village market[3] are included under informal education. For the purpose we use 0 and 1 values; 1 if any person in the family has contacted the extension officers, visited urban towns, listening to the transistors, or engaged in hand pounding of paddy and trading rice in the village market, and 0 if otherwise. The following cardinal numbers are alloted for different formal schooling statuses of the adult members of the family; O for illiterate and 1 for simple literate.[4] One point was given for each year of schooling. The overall educational score of the family is the horizontal sum of the scores allotted to the individual adult members of the family relating to the formal education and the scores allotted to the family as a whole relating to the individual items of informal learning.

Value-orientation score: Value-orientation as a socio-cultural attitude should receive due importance while studying the behavioural attitude of the tribals. Value refers simply to the "accepted or required behaviour for a person in a particular situation" (Cuber,

---

3. This is particularly practised by the tribal women. Despite being illiterate in the formal sense they can count the number up to 20 generally called, in the local dialect "Kori". They purchase paddy in the village/village market, prepare rice from paddy and sell them in the market and earn profit.

4. Simple literate persons are those who can atleast read and write his/her own name.

1959). In this study value-orientation of the tribal family is broadly classified into two groups viz. progressive value-orientation pattern and traditional value-orientation pattern. By progressive value-orientation, we mean those social and cultural norms which have appeal only to families who have a liking for success (i.e. materialistic) and the who are rational risk-takers and future-oriented. Traditional value-orientation, on the other hand, implies those social and cultural norms which have appeal only to those families who have a liking for security (i.e. non-materialistic) and who are risk-averters and past-oriented. Two attitudes namely the preference for accepting the developmental schemes offered by Government or any other agencies, and preference for including cash crops in their crop-portfolio, are taken to indicate their liking for success. The risk-taking attitude is roughly indicated by their preference for using the chemical fertilisers in growing the Kharif crops.[5] Similarly the preference of the family for sending their children to schools are taken to indicate their future orientations. If a family is found to have a liking for success (or security), risk-taker (or risk-averter) and future-oriented (or past-oriented) it is given one (or zero) point for each attitude. The horizontal sum of these points is taken to measure the value-orientation score of the family.

Total Annual Income: It is simply the total income of the family from agricultural and non-agricultural sources. The value of agricultural output[6] (total output from their own land and the share of output from the leased-in lands) at current prices is roughly taken to indicate the income from agriculture. The net money income from service and business (i.e. not salary from services and not profit from business activities) as well as wage-earnings[7] are taken into account

---

5. In fact the use of chemical fertilisers requires regulated water supply through secured irrigational facilities. In the absence of secure irrigational facilities, the farmers mostly grow Kharif crops under rain-fed situations. The use of chemical fertilisers in growing Kharif crops under such conditions involves risk in the sense that it might adversely affect the yield of the crops if rainfall does not occur in time and in sufficient amount.

6. That is, the sum of the product of the output of individual crops with their respective farm harvest prices.

7. Few cultivators in the village offer their services for agricultural use to others (besides doing their own agricultural works) and earn wage-income.

while estimating the income of the family from non-agricultural sources.

Simple correlation coefficient values are computed for measuring the extent of association between the educational score, value-orientation score and the average annual income of the households. The standard t-test has been employed for testing the significance value-orientation scores of the two sub-groups of households (taking total tribals into account) with high and low educational scores, also tested using the t-test.

Results and Discussion

We have computed the sex-wise literacy rates of the Oraon and Kharia tribes in the village and the results are presented in Table 1.

TABLE 1: **Sex-Wise Literacy Rate of the Oraon and Kharia Tribes in the Village**

Tribes	No. of households	No. of persons			No. of literate and educated persons			Literacy rate (in %)		
		(M)	(F)	(T)	(M)	(F)	(T)	(M)	(F)	(T)
Oraon (non-christian)	49	126	134	260	47	13	60	37.3	9.7	23.1
Oraon (Christian)	25	73	77	150	38	25	63	52.1	32.5	42.0
Oraon (Total)	74	199	211	410	85	38	123	42.7	18.0	30.0
Kharia (Total)	27	73	74	147	30	6	36	41.1	8.1	24.5
Grand total	101	272	285	557	115	44	159	42.3	15.4	28.5

Table 1 shows the literacy rate of the Oraon and Kharia tribes in the village. We find that the literacy rate is higher for the Oraon tribes (30.0%) as compared to that of the Kharia tribe (24.5%). Among the Oraon tribe the literacy rate is considerably higher for the Christian Oraon than the Non-Christian Oraon. In all the cases the literacy rates are higher for men than for women. On an average the literacy rates for men and women are 42.3% and 15.4% respectively. Owing to the obvious limitation of the literacy rate for measuring the degree of educational status of the person or family we have also computed the educational score for each household. The results relating to educational score along with the average value-orientation score and average annual income of the two tribes separately and also for the total are presented in Table 2.

TABLE 2: **Educational Score, Value-Orientation Score and Average Annual in come of the Tribal Households in the Village**

Tribes	No. of house-holds	Educat onal score		Value-orien-tation Score		Annual Income	
		Total	Average	Total	Average	Total	Average
Oraon (Non-Christian)	49	244	4.98	118	2.41	294428	6008.73
Oraon (Christian)	25	192	7.68	68	2.72	111570	4462.80
Oraon(Total)	74	436	5.89	186	2.51	405998	5486.46
Kharia	27	107	3.96	57	2.11	141900	5255.55
Grand Total	101	543	5.37	243	2.41	547890	5424.65

Table 2 shows the total and average educational scores, value-orientation scores and the annual income of the tribal households in the village. It is clear that the educational status of the Oraon tribes is higher than that of the Kharia tribe as indicated by the higher educational score for the Oraon tribe (5.89) than that of the average educational score for the Kharia tribe (3.96). The educational status of the Christian Oraon is higher than the educational status of the Non-Christian Oraon. The average value-orientation scores for the different categories of tribes show the same pattern of differences as that of the average educational scores. The average income of the Oraon tribe is also higher than the average annual income of the Kharia tribe. But unexpectedly the average annual income of the Christian Oraon, for which higher educational score and higher value-orientation has been noted, is considerably lower than the average annual income of the Non-Christian Oraon. This may be owing to their special socio-economic attitude. The Christian Oraons work hard for getting their livelihood, but as the money requirement for the bare necessities are fulfilled they prefer leisure than to work. It is worth noting in this context that the Christians in the village do not work at all for atleast 48 days (i.e. Sunday's) out of 365 days of the year.

TABLE 3: **Correlation Coeffeicents Between the Selected Indicators**

	Correlation Coefficient Between		
	ES & TI	VO & TI	ES & VO
-Oraon	0.599 * (0.358)	0.489 * (0.239)	0.548 * (0.300)
Kharia	0.728 * (0.529)	o.672 * (0.451)	0.634 * (0.401)
Total	0.624 * (0.389)	0.514 * (0.264)	0.573 * (0.328)

Notes:ES : Educational Score, VO : Value-Orientation Score TI : Total Annual Income

* : Significant at 0.1 percent level of significance

Figures in percentages are square of the correlation coefficient (i.e. r^2).

Table 3 shows the correlation coefficients between the educational, social and economic indicators. We have computed the correlation coefficient (r) between educational score and average annual income, value-orientation and average annual income and educational score and value-orientation score. We have also computed the r^2 - values (the so-called coefficient of determination) and presented with the r-values. We find significantly positive association between the educational score and the average annual income in all the cases of Oraon, Kharia and total tribes. On an average about 38.9 percent of the total variation in the average income of the tribal households is explained by the variation in the educational status of the households as indicated by the r^2 values. This might indicate direct effect of education on economic conditions of the tribals. We also find positive association between educational status and value-orientation on the one hand and positive association between value-orientation and economic condition on the other. Computed r-values are highly significant at 0.1 percent level of significance. This may be taken to indicate the indirect effect of education on economic condition through its impact on the value-orientation. In fact, the educational status determines the level of economic condition of the tribal people. As much as 26.4% of the total variation in the average income is explained by the value-orientation factor and the educational level explains about 32.8% of the total variation in the value-orientation as indicated by the r^2 values.

Further analysis of the data also indicates the role of education in determining the value system and economic condition of the tribal in rural areas. We have carried out the tests of significance of the difference in average income of the households with different levels (high vs. low) of education and value-orientation. For the purpose we have computed the difference, standard error of difference and the t-ratios[8] and results are presented in Table 4.

The results presented in Table 4 indicate that the average income of the group of household with high educational scores is significantly higher than the average income of the group of household with low educational scores. The results also indicate significantly different average income and average value-orientation score for the two groups of households with high vs. low value-orientation score and high vs. low educational score, respectively. The computed t-values are highly significant (ranging from 0.1% to 5.0% level of significance) in all cases. All these may be taken to indicate that the level of education significantly determines the level of value-

---

8. The formula used for computing the t-value is

$$t = \frac{X_1 - X_2}{\sqrt{(n_1 = 1)s_1^2} + \sqrt{(n_2 - 1)s_2^2}}$$

$$\frac{\sqrt{n_1 n_2 (n_1 + n_2 - 2)}}{n_1 + n_2}$$

Where n_1 &n_2 are the number of observations in the two subgroups with high & low scores respectively. X_1 & s_1^2 and X_2 & s_2^2 indicate the average values and their respective variance for the relevant items in the two sub-groups. The null hypothesis of equality of mean values in the two sub-groups is tested against the simple alternative of inequality in the mean values using two-tailed test.

orientation and the level of economic condition of the tribal people in rural areas.

TABLE 4: **Significance of the Difference in Average Income of the Households With Different Levels of Education and Value-orientation**

Items		Oraon	Kharia	Total
1. Significance of difference in the average income of the groups of households with high vs. low educational score	d	2457.87	4160.14	2846.40
	s.e.	567.93	1119.53	515.64
	t-value	4.33***	3.71**	5.62***
		(72)	(25)	(99)
2. Significance of difference in the average income of the groups of households with high vs. low value-orientation score.	d	2583.84	3168.16	2684.93
	s.e.	535.16	1175.51	495.37
	t-value	4.83***	2.69*	5.42***
		(72)	(25)	(99)
3. Significance of difference in the average value-orientation score of the groups of households with high vs. low educational score.	d	1.18	1.39	1.25
	s.e.	0.1839	0.3822	0.1690
	t-value	6.42***	3.64**	7.39***
		(72)	(25)	(99)

Notes: (i) The number of households with high vs. low educational score/value-orientation score for Oraon, Kharia and Total tribals are determined on the basis of higher or lower scores than their respective average scores.

(ii) Figures in parentheses below the t-values are respective degrees of freedom.

d : Difference in the mean values i.e. $\bar{X}_1 - \bar{X}_2$

s.e : Standard error of the difference.

*** : Significant at 0.1 percent level of significance

** : Significant at 1.0 percent level of "

* : Significant at 5.0 percent -do- "

Conclusions

The study indicates higher literary rate as well as higher educational status for the Oraon tribe, particularly the Christian-Oraon, as compared to that of the Kharia tribe. The social and economic status of the Oraon tribe is also better than that of the Kharia tribe. We find significantly positive association between the educational status and economic condition of the tribal households. Significantly positive association between the value-orientation and economic condition and educational status and value-orientation are also indicated. The results presented in this study sufficiently indicate the direct and indirect role of education in determining the economic conditions of the tribals in rural Chotanagpur. The study re-emphasizes the need of education as an important infrastructure for the economic development of the tribals. The adult and informal education programme with emphasis on training for the successful use of the new agricultural practices[9] followed by package of scheme assuring sufficient availability of the necessary agricultural infrastructure, may be of great help in this direction.

ACKNOWLEDGEMENT

The author is thankful to Dr. S. N. Sinha, Professor and Head of the Department of Economics, Ranchi University, Ranchi for comments and suggestions and to Sri K. B. Mahto for his assistance in data collection.

REFERENCES

1.Bhagat, L.N. (1981): "Adoption of New Agricultural Practices in Tribal Bihar - The View from a Village", The Economic Studies, Vol.22, No.2

2._______(1983.a): An Investigation of Supply Responses in Agriculture and their Differentials in a Backward/Economy-Chotanagpur Region, Unpublished Ph.D. Thesis, Calcutta University, Calcutta.

3._______(1983.b): "New Technology and Agricultural Development in Tribal Areas - A Study of Chotanagpur Region", in S.N. Sharma and Bhupinder Singh (eds.) Tribal Area Development, Society, for the Study of Regional Disparities, New Delhi.

4.Bougaert, V.D. Michael, (1975): "Training Tribal Enterpreneurs-An Experience in Social Change", Social Change, March-June

5.Cuber, J.F. (1959): Sociology: A Synthesis of Principles, Appleton Century-Crofts, Inc., New York.

6.Dutta, K.(1967): The Life and Thought of the People of Bihar, Scientific Book Agency, Calcutta.

7.Deogaokar, S.G. (ed.) (1979): Problems of Development of Tribal Areas, Leeladevi Publications, Delhi.

---

9. The use of chemical fertilisers by the tribal farmers of Chotanagpur, without knowing the specific role and its nutrient value, is indicated in some recent studies like Bhagat (1981) and Xavier Institute of Social Service (1978).

8.Goswami, P.C. and Saikia, P.D. (1970): "Problems of Agricultural Development in Tribal Areas", Indian Journal of Agricultural Economics, Vol.25, No. 3, July-September.

9.Hoel, P.G. and Jessen, R.J. (1977): Basic Statistics for Business and Economics, John Wiley & Sons, New Delhi.

10.Hoselitz, B.F. (1960): Sociological Aspects of Economic Growth, Amerind Publishing Co. Pvt. Ltd., New Delhi

11.Ivern, F. (1969): Chotanagpur Survey, Indian Social Institute, New Delhi.

12.Panchmukhi, P.R. (1982): Education and Economic Development: A Systematic and an Empirical Perspective (mimeo). Key-note paper presented at the 3rd Annual Conference of the Karnataka Economic Society, Udupi.

13.Prasad, N. (1961): Land and People of Tribal Bihar, The Bihar Tribal Research Institute, Govt. of Bihar, Ranchi

14.Quraishi, M.A. (1974): "Tribal Development in the Fifth Plan", Kurukshetra, Vol.23, No.1, October,1.

15.Roy Burman, B.K and Sharma, P.S. (1970): "Tribal Agriculture in India", Indian Journal of Agricultural Economics, Vol.25, No.3, July-September.

16.Roy Chaudhury,P.C. (1976): Folklore of Bihar, National Book Trust, New Delhi.

17.Sachidananda (1964): "Social Change in Chotanagpur", Bulletin of the Tribal Research Institute, Vol. 6, No.2.

18.Sen, J.(1968): Community Development Chotanagpur, The Asiatic Society, Calcutta.

19.Sharma, B.D. (1984): Planning for Tribal Development, Prachi Prakashan, New Delhi.

20.Sinha, B.B. (1982): Society in Tribal India, Wiley Eastern Limited, New Delhi.

21.Singh, B. and Bhandari, J.S. (eds.) (1979): The Tribal World and its Transformation, Concept Publishing Company, New Delhi.

22.Srinivas, M.N., Seshaiah, S. and Parthasarthy, V.S. eds. (1977): Dimensions of Social Change in India, Allied Publishers Pvt. Ltd., New Delhi.

23.Vidyarthi,L.P. (1964): Cultural Contours of Tribal Bihar, Punthi Pustak, Calcutta.

24.Vidyarthi,L.P. (1971): Socio-Economic Implications of Industrialisation in India, Ranchi University, Ranchi.

25.Xavier Institute of Social Services (1978): Report of the Bench Mark Survey of Eleven Villages in Kanke and Ormanjhi Blocks of Ranchi District in Bihar, 1977-78, Ranchi (mimeo).

APPENDIX

The following table shows the caste-wise and occupation-wise number of households and population in the village:

	Number of households (population in Parentheses engaged mainly in		
	Cultivation	Agricultural labour	Total
Oraon (Non-Christian)	47 (257)	2 (3)	49 (260)
Oraon (Christian)	25 (150)	.. ..	25 (150)
Oraon Total	72 (407)	2 (3)	74 (410)
Kharia	25 (138)	2 (9)	27 (147)
Lohra	4 (26)	5 (24)	9 (50)
Mahli	1 (3)	4 (23)	5 (26)
Chik-Baraik	2 (6)	.. ..	2 (6)
Grand total	104 (508)	13 (59)	117 (639)

EIGHT

Tribal Health and Medicine: A Keynote Address

S. P. Gupta

A great deal of emphasis has been laid on human resources development in the approach document of the Planning Commission for the Seventh Five Year Plan 1985-90. The aspect of Tribal Health has been highlighted particularly in sections of the document devoted to development of scheduled castes and scheduled tribes. The National Health Policy enunciated that in the establishment of reorganised services, the first priority should be accorded to provide to those tribals residing in the hilly and backward areas as well as the endemic disease affected populations and the vulnerable sections of the society. The importance of the tribal health and medicine has to be appreciated in this context.

The normal health of the tribal people cannot be said to be bad but after infection their condition often becomes chronic. In earlier times there were some endemic diseases like Malaria, Tuberculosis, Leprosy etc. To these has been added growing under nourishment on account of dwindled resources. There is a diversity of environment in which the different tribal communities live. There are even today some small geographical pockets which are rich in natural resources affording plentiful vegetable and animal products like the one we have in Singhbhum district (Bihar). Such areas are, however, pitifully few. Most of the regions which tribals inhabit are now improvised. The great chunks of forests have disappeared resulting in soil erosion. The game is extinct. At many places, the land has been taken from the tribals for development projects. In this respect the remedy, of course a long term measure, lies in improvement of their basic economic condition providing them the means of income which will enable them to buy food materials.

Again, the primitive tribal communities have remained isolated from the rest of the society and their exposure to the modern world has been limited, the result being two fold. One: they had not contracted the diseases of the modern society, but may fall an easy prey to them once they come in more frequent contact with the members of modern society. Second: their physique is not used to allopathic system of medicine.

Tribal Concept of Health, Disease and Remedy

Tribal concept of health, disease, treatment, life and death is as varied as their culture. Accordingly, the tribal society is guided by traditionally laid down customs and every member of the society is expected to conform to it. The fate of individual and the community at large, depends on their relationship with unseen forces which intervene human affairs. If men offend them, the mystical powers punish by sickness, death or other natural calamities.

Disease is caused by bad spirits and the spirits are bad either because one has not properly propitiated them. Thus, to a tribal mind, the real enemies of human health and prosperity are the gods and the dead. The usual theory of disease in tribal society is that it is caused by the breach of some taboo or by hostile spirits, ghosts or the dead. Sickness is the routine punishment for every lapse and crime meted out to them by the spirits. Accordingly they have taboos and prayers. The "pahan" (village priest) in addition to his religious functions acts as the mediator between the people and the mystical powers. By propitiations and prayers he tries for the good relationship between the people on one hand and maintain mystical powers on the other which intervene human affairs. Thus, magico-religious treatment of disease is resorted to. As a matter of fact, disease to a tribal mind is like another phenomenon of the natural world, is many faced and essentially incomprehensible in the sense that no single theory will cover all the known facts perfectly.

Tribal Traditional Beliefs and Practices

The Santhal has a theory of disease which in its scientific view point is as natural a cause as infection caused by bacteria. But we can look upon as an agency which is natural and yet supernatural and sometimes also diffused with human agency. According to them, disease would be caused by a 'Tijo' (Bodding-1925), which may be large or very microscopic. These 'Tijos' are located in different parts of the body. 'Tijos' enter the body through food etc., and cause leprosy or hydrophobia and other diseases. The 'Tijo' germs are often believed to be collected by witches for spreading diseases.

The Santhal has a belief that evil men by dint of their magical power intrude dirts such as stone or wood or pebbles or lumps of hair in the body which cause unbearable pain. The 'Ojha' sucks out from the body these things and they believe that by doing so their pain is cured.

Besides, the Santhal have a horde of *Bongas* or spirits which are malevolent ones actively intervening their affairs. They believe that these Bongas or spirits have control over the various natural phenomena and the natural calamities those often occur, are because of their influence. They, therefore always try to appease them through magico-religious practices.

In fact the relation between the Santhal and the Bongas is one of reverential fear, dependence, submission and propitiation. The Bongas are worshipped and propitiated with the sacrifice of animals, offering of rice, beer and the blood of the sacrificial animal. Troisi (1978) while analysing the worship of Bongas of the Santhal, considered two interrelated aspects: the instrumental and the expressive.

"On the one hand the performance of the religious rites expressed the recognition of the existence of the supernatural powers that can be exercised by the bongas. On the other hand, the powers of the bongas are generally invoked to secure the goodwill of the beneficient ones and to avert the ill-will of the malificient ones. In other words, the instrumental aspect behind these religious rites expresses an alliance with the benevolent bongas and through them control of harmful spirits. The expressive aspect is symbolised and manifested in a special manner in the various seasonal rites and festivals correlated to the annual agricultural and the recurring rites of passage".

The Malpaharias, the Saurias and other Pahariyas of the Rajmahal hill of the Santhal Parganas in Bihar also believe that one of the causes of disease is the intrusion of the bits of stone or wood, etc., by sorcerer and which is cured by sucking out these things from the body.

The Oraon sorcerer carries sometimes with him a rag bundle containing what are known as "Nasans" (destructive and harmful agencies) and include human hair, nail pairings, claws, fragments of bone and legs of chickens and other birds and animals and also small quantities of rice grains, mustard seeds and certain other grains. Sorcerer mixes these in the food pouncing appropriate spells which kill the victim. The Oraon have a belief that there are among them some powerful sorcerers or witches who by some appropriate mantras extract the liver of an intended victim without the latter perceiving it.

The Hos of Singhbhum believe that women dying in child birth transform themselves into malignant spirits and delay in delivery as also other complications. Children suffer from rickets owing to the influence of spirits who are but the disengaged souls of dead children. The Hos also believe in witch known as 'Rakti Bhawani' which shoots arrows at night.

The Kharia of Dalbhum believe in spirit basis of disease. The Korwás believe that fever in women and children are caused by 'Churail' which is a female spirit and extremely mischievous.

The Birhor (Uthln) takes up some arwa rice in his hand and invokes his 'Nasan' spirit and throws the rice in the direction of the enemy (house) and injures him.

The Asur call them 'Dabia' or 'Bishaha'. They are supposed to exercise evil influence.

According to S.C. Roy (1912:486) "The Mundas are great believers in the power of evil-eye, and in cases of repeated sickness in a family or among the cattle of a family a witch-finder: The Sokha, Mati or Bhagat is appealed for detecting the witch. "Thus, the Mundas have a doctrine concerning sickness and functioning groups of curers. They also attribute a few diseases to particular deity as for instance, epidemic diseases like cholera, smallpox etc., are attributed to "Sitals". With an effort to avert the diseases, they annually worship the deity. The belief of the interference of supernatural agency in diseases, the attribution of some diseases to certain deities and the belief in evil eye, spirit possession or sorcery clearly indicate that still the Mundas have clung to their traditional modes of beliefs and practices.

Tribal Pharmacopoeia

There are many natural remedies, decoctions of forest herbs of healing lotions known to the tribals. That means the tribal people have pharmacopoeia of their own for their manifold diseases like malaria, Yaws, leprosy, scabies, venereal diseases, bowel complaints, influenze, opthalmia, Cholera, Smallpox, etc.

Although now there are Block dispensaries and mobile hospitals, but the tribal people mainly depend for prevention and cure of their disease on their traditional medicinemen. The author (1974 and 1980) described some of the herbal remedies used by the tribals in Chotanagpur and Native Medicinal uses of plants by the Asurs of Netarhat Plateau (Bihar) respectively.

Regarding the origin of the large number of medicines, practically nothing is known. The remedies resorted to in various diseases are quite startling. The tribals have hit upon some herb in some way or another and found it efficacious. They have then tried the same for complaints other than those it was originally used for, and have in this way, been guided by experience. But their uses are not so far recorded in literature or at least that particular medicinal property which the tribals attribute to the plants is not known.

To a tribal mind all fevers are alike and he hardly makes any difference between simple fever, malarial fever, pneumonia fever, typhoid fever, influenza etc. Similarly, he treats all stomach pains on the same footing whether it is dysenteric pain or constipation or some other intestinal disorder. So far as diagonosis of the disease is concerned, the tribals face great difficulty, particularly when they are confronted with anything different from the common disease of every day occurence.

Suggestions

In 1982, the Ministry of Health and Family Welfare constituted a committee to undertake a review of the existing health and related problems in tribal areas and to evolve suggestions in respect of genetic, medicare, public health, community health, problems of the scheduled tribes. However, few suggestions may be made here:

1. Incidence of tuberculosis, yaws, veneral diseases, malaria, leprosy, goitre and anaemia is high in some tribal areas. Specific surveys to know the incidence of various diseases and dimensions of the problem are desirable.

2. Very little attention has been given on the tribal system of medicine which appears to be a mix of herbal practices, ritualism and witchcraft. Adequate research into this system is desirable to derive benefits from it. In as much as herb medicine is associated with sorcery, magic and superstition, it may be discarded since its effects may be more imaginary than real. On the other hand, scientific investigations of some herbs may reveal important curative properties.

3. Medicinal herbs and plants grow in abundance in the tribal areas which are getting denuded on account of pressure on land and destruction of forests. It is also feared that with their progressive exposure to modernisation, this great treasure may be lost in due course. Therefore, there is an urgent need for Botanists, Anthropologists, Biochemists and Medical Scientists to swing into action immediately and collect information regarding plants used by the tribals as food, medicines, fibre and for aesthetic purposes with particular reference to those used to effect the reproductive process and as stabilisers of age.

4. There is a treasure of medical knowledge in the minds of tribal medicine man. Generations of tribals have sought medical relief through this knowledge. Special research centres may be established to identify, consolidate and document this knowledge so that it is not

lost to posterity for ever.

5. There is widespread use of herbs, leaves, roots etc., among tribals and some of them are used in the Ayurvedic, Unani, Homeopathic and Allopathic systems also. As such, active encouragement may be given to their cultivation and use.

6. The relaxed norms for population coverage by PHCS and sub-centres, i.e., one Primary Centre (PHC) for a population of 20,000 and one sub-centre for a population of 3000 need to be established in tribal areas.

7. Concomitantly, prophylactic and curative measures have to be mounted in specific health fields. Attention has to be directed more towards prophylaction, safe drinking water, sanitation and hygiene.

Recently Sri Rajiv Gandhi, Prime Minister of India has sent directives to the Chief Ministers to personally monitor the implementation of the Welfare Programme for Weaker Sections. He emphasized that national integration was best promoted by ensuring that every citizen, irrespective of caste, creed, language or religion, was able to fully participate in all spheres of national activity without any discrimination. It is in this perspective that the foregoing measures outlined under Tribal Health and Medicine for the welfare of scheduled tribes should be viewed.

REFERENCES

1. Biswas,P.C. 1934: Concept of Disease among the Primitive People of India. Journal of Department, Letters, University of Calcutta, Vol. XXV, pp. 1-28.
2. Bodding, P.O. 1925: Studies in Santal Medicine and connected folklore-I. The Santals and Disease, Mem. Asiatic Soc. Bengal, Vol.X(I), pp.1-132.
3. Gupta, S.P. 1974: Tribes of Chotanagpur Plateau: An Ethno-Nutritional and Pharmacological Cross-Section, Bihar Tribal Welfare Research Institute, Ranchi.
4. Gupta, S.P. 1980: Native Medicinal uses of plants by the Asurs of Netarhat Plateau (Bihar), Glimpses of Indian Ethnobotary, pp.218-231. Oxford & IBH Publishing Co.
5. Jain, S.K. 1979: Medicinal Plants, National Book Trust of India, 3rd Ed., New Delhi.
6. Ray, U.K., A.K., Das & S.K. Basu 1982: To be with Santals, Govt. of West Bengal, Calcutta.
7. Roy, S.C. 1912: The Mundas and their Country, Calcutta.
8. Roy, S.C. 1915: The Oraons of Chotanagpur, Ranchi.

9. Roy, S.C. 1925: The Birhors, Ranchi
10. Troisi, J. 1978: Tribal Religion, New Delhi, Manohar Publications.
11. —— 1984: Report of the working groups on Development of Scheduled Tribes during Seventh Five Year Plan 1985-90, Govt. of India, Ministry of Home Affairs, New Delhi.

NINE

Health Condition and Nutritional Status Among the Bhil and Garasia - Two Tribes of Rajasthan

M. Haque

We are living in a country where malnutrition is common. Even today crores of people are suffering from growing hunger, incomplete mental and physical developments, lack of energy and susceptibility to diseases.

Development is the essence of life and government has given highest importance for tribal development. The elements of health and growth are vital aspects of any developmental plan. The impact of both planned and spontaneous development programme will have its impact on the aspect of health and growth. Sometime, the mobility of the population and desire of the progress are seen through the spectrum of health and growth. Here in this paper three important indices of the body built have been shown, also an attempt has been made to ascertain the health condition and nutritional status of the two important tribal populations of Rajasthan namely the Bhil and the Garasia through anthropometric study.

Area of Study

Udaipur - The territory now known as district Udaipur used to be a part of former Mewar State. In April 1948, it was united with the state of Rajasthan. After the merger, a separate district of Udaipur was formed. It is situated in between 23.46' and 26.20' North latitude and 73.00' and 74.35' East longitude. The Udaipur district is surrounded in North by Ajmer and Pali, in South Dungarpur and Banswara, East by Bhilwara and West by Pali and Srohi district. It has eight tehsils. The district consists of an elevated plateau on the north and fertile land on the east. South-Western part is covered by rocks, hills and dense forests. The Aravalli range enters the district in Bhim from Ajmer district. Climate is moderate and generally healthy. Rocks of districts consist for most part of schists belonging to the Aravalli system, rich in minerals. About 10 percent of the total classified area was under forest. Altitude of Udaipur is 3,000 feet above the sea level.

Material and Method

Bhil and the Garasia are the major tribal populations of Rajasthan. Data on 123 Bhils and 111 Garasias of Udaipur district constitute the materials of the paper. Standard technique and tables have been followed. Both Bhils and Garasias are agricultural group but Garasias are more competent agriculturists, whom they consider as one step superior in social hierarchy as they are the offspring of Bhil woman and Rajput man and as the Bhils are beef eaters. Rice, wheat and maize are the staple food of the community, pulses are consumed adequately and consumption of nonleafy vegetables are not limited. Occasionally, they take animal protein, milk and milk products and fruits also. Frequently, they take liquour. Consumption of leafy vegetables is inadequate.

Result and Discussion

Table 1 shows the stature distribution of the studied groups. It is evident that the Bhils are taller than the Garasias. Both the groups show significant difference (3.76) in the character. But when the sitting height vertex is considered the Garasia shows higher mean value, there exists nonsignificant (0.74) difference in this character. In chest circumference Bhil shows higher value and there exists significant difference (8.33) with Garasia. But when the height is considered it is evident that Garasias are heaver than the Bhils. They also exhibit significant (4.36) differences in this regard.

Three indices of the body build of the adult studied groups have been calculated from appropriate direct physical measurements and have been shown in the following paragraph. These measurements are Stature, Sitting Height Vertex, Chest Circumference and weight.

1. **Body Build Index or Pignet Index**: It is expressed by formula:

Stature - (Chest Circumference in Cms + Weight in Kgs)

Body built according to this index is noted (Pignet 1901) as:

Very Sturdy	up to 10
Sturdy	10 - 15
Good	16 - 20
Average	21 - 25
Weak	26 - 30
Very weak	31 - 35
Poor	36 & above.

2. **Pelidisi or Von Parquet Index**: It is the relationship between sitting height and weight which is expressed by the formula:

$$\sqrt[3]{\frac{10 \times Weight\,(Gr)}{Sitting\ Height\,(Cms)}} \times 100$$

Masson (1931) stated that for small children a *pelidisi* of 100 represent, the ideal. It has since been found that for adults a value somewhat less than this, probably 97 or 98 represent the normal state of nutrition. Whatever opinion one has with regard to quantitative significance of the *pelidisi index* one can assume that westerness at least a *Pelidisi* around 90 represent a distinctly low state of nutrition, and a *Pelidisi* over 100 (sometime value as high as 112, 113 have been found) usually represent a fat person.

So the nutritional state according to the index can be rated thus:

up to 92	:	distinctly low state of nutrition
92.1-95	:	State of mild under nutrition.
95.1-100	:	Normal State of nutrition.
100.1-105	:	Mildly over weight.
105.1-above	:	Distinctly over weight or obese.

3. **Korperfulla Index**: It is the relationship between standing height and weight as is indicated by the formula:

100x Weight in grams/(Height in Cms.)^3

Though this index is used for comparing the body build of different population groups, it has not been much applied in making very reliable assesment of physique or nutritional state of individuals or groups. Based on available data on the index, nutritional state in terms of *Korperfulla index* can be rated thus:

up to 1.2	:	From low state of malnutrition to very mild state of under nutrition.
1.21-1.5	:	Normal or satisfactory state of nutrition.
1.51-1.6	:	Mildly or moderately over weight.

Both Bhils and Garasias are short statured people, their average height being 1636.17±6.00 and 1616.67±5.14 respectively, and Bhils are taller and lighter than the Garasias. Physique and nutritional state as indicated by the median values of the three indices are very weak. According to the Pignets Body Build Index, only two Bhil men have the body build that may be termed as very sturdy and sturdy (0.81 percent each), 2.44 percent of the Bhils are good, 87.81 percent of the Bhil have weak to poor body build. There is not a single Garasia who has either very sturdy or sturdy body build. Only 2.70 percent have the good and 87.39 percent have weak to poor body build. The distribution of the *Pelidisi* and *Korperfulla* indices of the studied groups show that 21.14 percent of Bhils are under nourished and 80.49 percent are malnourished. The 14.14 percent of the Garasias are undernourished and 78.38 percent are malnourished. It is also noticed that 6.50 percent of the Bhils and 4.50 percent of the Garasias are in obese condition. Rest were in normal nutritional state. The nutritional status of the people under study as reflected by the above indices can be said to be on the whole unsatisfactory.

Summary

To sum up, it can be stated that asthenic is predominant in all the groups. Their body build reflects that it is due to inadequate and unsatisfactory diet which is poor both in quality and quantity, deficient in calories and protein. The food of the people depends on soil, supply, taboo related to food and cultural constraints. But here the malnutrition and undernutrition is due to mainly non-availability of food and partly to a lesser extent to the cultural constraint. The nutritional status of the studied groups as reflected by three indices of body build (*Pignet index*, *Pelidisi index* and *Korperfulla Index)* have been found to be on the whole unsatisfactory. Under these circumstances they should be inspired to take more nutritive foods like animal protien, milk, milk products, green vegetables and fruits which are easily available in the locality.

It is clear and well accepted fact that there exists a large gap between different population of tribals and between tribals and non tribals also. We cannot expect national integration unless there is uniformity in developmental programme, may be the case of health injustice or economical disparity? The paper reveals the fact to the galaxy of experts here as to how to have justice in the light of National Integrity and tribal development when these people are on a threat of health hazard.

Acknowledgment

The author expresses his sincere gratitude to the Director, Anthropological Survey of India, for providing all facilities for this investigation and thanks to all others associated with this paper.

REFERENCE

Mason E.D. & Bendict F.G. 1931 : The Basal Metabolism of South Indian Women. Ind. Jr. Med. Res. 19 - 752

Pignet Du 1901 : Quoted by Krogman W.M. Growth of Man (1941) II.

TABLE 1 : **Stature**

Group	No	Range	Mean ± SE	SD ± SE	CV ± SE
Bhil	123	1435-1854	1636.17± 6.00	66.64± 4.25	4.07± 0.25
Garasia	111	1494-1722	1616.57± 5.14	54.15± 3.63	3.34± 0.22

TABLE -2 :**Sitting Height Vertex**

Group	No	Range	Mean ± SE	SD ± SE	CV ± SE
Bhil	123	714-891	785.15± 3.23	35.85± 2.28	4.56± 0.29
Garasia	111	692-855	790.40± 1.83	29.86± 2.00	3.77± 0.25

TABLE -3 :**Chest Circumference**

Group	No	Range	Mean ± SE	SD ± SE	CV ± SE
Bhil	123	658-888	815.27± 3.26	36.23± 2.31	4.44± 0.28
Garasia	111	696-912	795.15± 3.51	36.98± 2.48	4.65± 10.3

TABLE 4 :**Weight**

Group	No	Range	Mean ± SE	SD ± SE	CV ± SE
Bhil	123	30-62	46.03± 0.49	5.47± 0.34	11.88± 0.75
Garasia	111	36-60	47.25± 0.48	5.09± 0.34	10.77± 0.72

TABLE 5 :**Body Build Index**

Group	No	Range	Median
Bhil	123	9 - 69	36.09
Garasia	111	15 - 51	34.90

TABLE 6 :**Body Build Index Classification**

Class	Range	Bhil		-	Garasia
		No	Percent	No	Percent
Very sturdy	-10	1	0.81	-	-
Sturdy	11-15	1	0.81	-	-
Good	16-20	3	2.44	3	2.70
Medium	21-25	10	8.13	11	9.91
Weak	26.30	26	21.14	19	17.12
Very Weak	31-35	27	21.95	25	22.52
Poor	36-	55	44.72	53	47.75
Total	-	123	100.00	111	100.00

TABLE 7 :**Pelidist Index**

Group	No	Range	Median
Bhil	123	86.07-110.10	98.33
Garasia	111	86.46-106.23	98.42

TABLE 8 :**Pelidist Index Classification**

Class	Range	Bhil No	Bhil Percent	Garasia No	Garasia Percent
Distinctly low state of nutrition	-92.0	11	8.94	7	6.31
State of mild under nutrition	29.1-95.0	26	21.14	16	14.14
Normal state of nutrition	95.1-100.0	58	47.16	54	48.65
Mildly over weight	100.1-105.0	20	16.26	29	26.13
Distinctly over weight	105.1-	8	6.50	5	4.50
Total	-	123	100.00	111	100.00

TABLE 9: **Korperfulla Index**

Group	No	Range	Median
Bhil	123	0.61-1.65	1.06
Garasia	111	0.63-1.64	1.11

TABLE 10: **Korperfulla Index Classification**

Class	Range	Bhil No	Bhil Percent	GARASIA No	GARASIA Percent
Low state of mal nutrition to very mild state of under nutrition	-1.20	99	80.49	87	78.38
Normal or satisfactory state of nutrition	1.21-1.50	23	18.70	23	20.72
Mildly or moderately over weight	1.51-1.60	1	0.81	1	0.90
TOTAL		123	100.00	111	100.00

TEN

Indigenous Health Practices and Its Problems: A Study Among the Bhoksas of Nainital

A. K. Chaudhury and M.H.R. Khashmisi

Introduction

The Thirtieth World Health Assembly decided in 1977 that by the year 2000, people of all countries should have a level of health that would permit them to lead socially and economically productive lives. To achieve this target among the tribal people in all parts of India will be difficult to reach if not impossible, owing to the major obstacle of persuading all of them to come for medical treatment as they themselves have a traditionally developed system of diagnosis and cure. In many tribal societies it is considered that the disease is caused by the hostile spirits and ghosts of the dead. They also believe that such spiritually caused disease must be cured spiritually. This kind of faith is deterrent to many who would otherwise have visited the dispensaries or hospitals for modern medical treatment.

In the present paper an attempt will be made to provide a brief description of some of the magical therapies prevalent among the Bokshas living in the Nainital district of Uttar Pradesh, for curing some diseases and even dog-bite which will reflect their century-old faith in indigenous healing practices. The social relevance and valuable psychological aspect of such tribal methods of diagnosis and cure is also highlighted. Considering the present poor state of general health conditions of the tribe, some suggestions are offered which may help to bring them under the fold of proper medical treatment to improve their health.

The Community

The Bhoksas are one of the five Scheduled tribes of Uttar Pradesh, and are chiefly concentrated in the districts of Nainital, Bijnor and Dehradun. They trace their origin to the legendary Jagdeo of Dharnagar or Rajput nobles of Jaipur and Jodhpur who had to migrate after heroic battles with the Moghuls to 'Tarai' tract. The Bhoksas of Dehradun are also known as 'Mahra' or 'Mehre' who were used by Raja of Tehri Garhwal as guides during hunting because of their intimate knowledge of forest. Hassan (1971), however, keeps the view that the Bhoksas belong to Mongoloid ethnic groups. According to Crooke (1896) in the Garhwal area the 'Bhoksas' or 'Bhogsa' is the name for sorcerer.

Role of magicman

The people of Bhoksa community living in the district of Nainital seek treatment for all kinds of ailments from the magicman known as *Bharara* who is also considered to be well aware of medicinal values of locally available herbs. They are also worshipers of Goddess *Kashipur Wali Devi* or Durga, and therefore regarded as a possessor of divine powers.

According to Shri Prem Singh; an old, aged and noted *Bharara* living in the Barheni village of Bazpur tehsil of Nainital district, diseases may occur due to both disfunction of body such as fever, Cholera, dysentery etc., and also due to the influence of supernatural agencies like spirits, ghosts and local deities. Some specific symptoms for diagnosing the diseases originating from supernatural agencies are: unrythmic and abrupt movements of pulse, restlessness, swelling with ache and convulsive movements in stomach, general health weakness, sudden violent body movements, paralysis of organ or of body parts, unconsciousness, fever etc.

For the treatment of various diseases, recitation of mantras, locally known as "*Jharan - Lagana*", is essential although some times *Bharara* also prescribes certain herbs and roots. The curative procedures of dog-bite and some other ailments described by the said *Bharara* are mentioned below :

1. *Dog-bite*

Twenty one mud balls are required. *Bharara* will then recite mantra and pick up those balls one after another and move his hand from left to right direction around his head. This process will be repeated thrice in the morning, evening and next day morning or till the poison ends. After such act when the balls will be broken the hair of a dog will appear which will be of same colour of the dog which bit. As soon as the patient is cured, he should offer one *Bheli of Gur* to *Kashipur Wali Devi*. No restriction is imposed on eating and no special prayer is to be offered.

2. *Jaundice (Pilia)*

The disease is identified by symptoms. One *Katora* (small vessel) of mustard oil and ten small bunches of *Durba Grass* is required. Patients sit before the *Bharara* who then holds the *Katora* in front of the face and while shaking the grass he will recite mantras. One *Bheli of Gur* is to be offered to Devi after patient is cured.

3. *Abscess (Gambhir)*

One mud ball after reciting mantra will be handed over to patient and he will be instructed to touch the ball with abscess after every 2-3 hours. After 2 days abscess will be cured.

4. *Half side headache (Adhsiri)*

Before day break in the morning the patient will visit the *Bharara*, who with the help of a knife draw a figure on the ground. The side on which headache is felt will be repeatedly scratched while reciting mantra.

Apart from above *Bharara* has also informed us about the medicinal value of *Harjori* leaves; the juice of which can cure bone fracture, and also some other herbs which are used to prepare medicine to cure diseases like leucoderma, eye diseases, stoppage of menstruation, infertility etc. Normally *Bharara* for his services do not accept anything in cash or kind but patient usually after cure give community feast. The *Bharara* was, however, found concerned about the present situation of non-availability of herbs caused by rapid deforestation.

To assess the impact and success of such indigeneous health practices, contacts were made with the individuals who have been treated earlier. It is observed that Shri Jagan Singh living in the Kela bandwari village; a victim of dog-bite in the past, is leading a healthy life and Shri Guman Singh of same village has shown the mark of large abscess healed after the magical treatment. Majority of them interviewed have expressed deep faith in their indigenous health practices and also informed that they first of all consult *Bharara* for the treatment of every kind of diseases. A few among them, however, keep the view that the magical power of *Bharara's* mantras are now not so effective as it was in the past.

The Psychological Aspect

The success of healing treatment of magic-man in a tribal society like Bhoksas probably lies on its valuable psychological function and on its social acceptance. It is an established fact that many diseases are caused partly due to mental cause. For instance, anxiety may cause peptic ulcers, guilt or fear may cause indigestion and frustration may cause constipation. Whenever, in a tribal society a patient feels that he is ill because a ghost or spirit has attacked him, the magic-man removes his fear and restores confidence by appeasing the offended spirit. Thus his act promotes 'will to live' which is one of the most important needs in a case of serious illness.

General health status

The general health condition of the Bhoksa tribe, however, does not reveal a satisfactory picture as the incidences of Tuberculosis and stomach disorders were found quite frequently. Many children suffer from skin infections and have shown the sign of malnutrition. Such a situation, is not unique in Bhoksa tribe since there are several other tribes in India who suffer from one or another form of such grave health problems.

This kind of observation further reflects the weaknesses of indigeneous health practices which have to be replaced soon by the modern medicine in order to achieve better health.

We understand modern medicine as a system of curing based on scientific techniques and rational concepts of cause and effect. Unfortunately the doctors who shoulder the responsibilities of promoting such modern medicine in the tribal areas just partly determine the total range of practices involved in treatment and cure. They probably fail to realise that their treatment is embedded in social as well as scientific martix. Efforts should therefore be made to fit the practice of medicine to a role that is appropriate to social system of the tribal people.

To begin with, doctors may start taking interest to understand the tribal methods of diagnosis and cure instead of completely ignoring them. If necessary, they can also invite tribal magic-men and allow them to perform magical rituals for his patients which will act as a kind of faith healing and psychological treatment. For such act of kindness, on the other hand, doctors will achieve respect as well as confidence of tribal people since they will feel that their cultural values are not neglected.

Another possible way would be to recruit educated tribal boys and girls as health staffs who will be able to understand their own affairs promptly. Such health staffs will not only explain the essential aspects of health and hygiene, but will also be able to help medical authority to take assistance of local magic-man in case any patient needs so. By such efforts we can make tribal people feel that they can also make a contribution to their own community and to their country at large which will be an important aspect of their integration.

ELEVEN

Health Status of Korwas: A Case Study

A. N. Sandhwar

Poverty is a curse for any one but it is more than that for the Korwa tribe of Madhya Pradesh. There are two types of Korwa: one major group who live in hills and another at plains. In recent years, their miseries have been more aggravated. The ban of the shifting cultivation has further added miseries to them because no suitable substitute for their livelihood has been provided by the Government or any one. The deteriorating health and drinking water problems are one of the main causes of decrease in their population.

The Korwa who has been socially disregarded and branded as "Jungli" dirty man and now further being cut off from the main stream of social life because of a new type of disease "Khujli" with which the Korwas are mainly affected in and around Bagicha area. Hardly any Korwa is found without the disease. Because of this nobody wants to come in contact with them and they are getting withdrawn far away from the regional social life.

This disease is perhaps mainly because of acute water problem in the "Pat" area and lack of clothes. The main source of water is stream or "Nalahs". It is being used for bathing, cleaning, drinking etc., on Pat area. Ahirs are in good number and they have kept good number of milking cattle for milk business. They clean their cattle in the same stream from which the Korwa use for drinking and other purposes. The water further gets polluted because the Korwa keep slices of "Galtra" and" Konda" in the running water for demantling its bitterness.

Here, I would like to inform that *galtra* and *Konda* are the main types of fresh edible products. It is reported that because of polluted water they are having the skin disease. It was found that the scarcity of clothes is further cause of this disease. It is said that a cloth which one wears gets torn on their body. There is no question of regular bath and changing of the clothes periodically. It is not because that they do not want to take bath regularly or they do not want to live cleanly, rather they cannot afford to take regular bath. On survey it was found that out of 40 Korwas 36 had only one set of clothes, 3 had only 1 shirt extra and only 1 had 2 sets of clothes. Again among 40 female Korwas 33 had one set of clothes to wear. The rest had two saris. This survey shows that they are not only suffering from skin diseases but also they are socially avoided.

Another disease which is very serious is called *Rangbad* : it is a serious and fatal disease. It begins with the symptom of cramping of the hands and legs. Then there is tension in nerves and further gets paralysis in leg and hand. It is painful one and one, dies within one hour. Five cases of such deaths have been recorded in Bagicha area and out of which 4 are the Korwas in 1983.

Besides it, large cases of cough, leprosy, malaria have been reported. The improper care by the Government has added to their suffering. How to talk about National Integration, when they are being cut off from even at regional and village level.

Therefore, in view of the serious situation there is an urgent need of proper medical survey and eradication programme to be taken at war footing.

TWELVE

The Role of Developmental Agencies In a Tribal Area

Dipesh Chaudhury & S. K. Pal

India is a vast country with mosaic topology and varied environments. It harbours very many tribal cultures, sub-cultures, languages and religions. In order to attempt developing tribal area especially the economy of the tribals, an interested administrator should essentially possess an intimate knowledge about the concerned tribal society first before he wants to float any developmental scheme or programme for any tribal area. Tribal development categorically means the welfare of a particular group of people who have been identified as "Tribe" in our Constitution. It is the overall welfare of these people covering all aspects of life, like; social, cultural, economical, educational and also some such other relevant items that are directly or indirectly connected with fulfilling or optimising life situations and aspirations.

In this paper an attempt has been made firstly to identify and ascertain how the various agencies have undertaken programmes among the Juang tribe inhabiting Keonjhar district, of Orissa in order to raise the standard of economy, education, health and sanitation and secondly, how far these agencies have been successful to motivate them or to develop new taste for them to accept the developmental schemes of those agencies.

Various agencies both Government and non-Government are working at Juangpirh of Keonjhar district. They are the Juang Development Agency (JDA), Large Size Agricultural Multipurpose Co-operative Society (LAMPS), Village Reconstruction Organisation (VRO) etc. Among these, JDA's contribution is most significant. The JDA's administrative office was set up in 1978 in Keonjhar district town and the office of the project site is at Gonasika, about 50 km away from Keonjhar town.

In the tribal dialect, Juang means 'Man'. Sometimes the neighbourers call the Juang as Pattua, meaning the wearer of leaf dress, though leaf dress has long been given up by them. The typical Juang villages are situated on hill tops or slopes, surrounded by hills and forest. Generally the houses are situated under the branches of mango or Jackfruit trees.

For assessing the welfare programme of the various agencies, field investigation was carried out in Keonjhar district, Orissa during January - March, 1985. The following aspects were investigated for study:

1. Economical upliftment programme
2. Educational Programme and
3. Health and Sanitation programme.

Programmes for Economic Upliftment

The Juangpirhs of Keonjhar district are primarily surrounded by the hills and mountain ranges where practice of settled agriculture is practically difficult. The major part of the area is covered with dense forest and the area is infested with different types of wild games. Sometimes the hill slopes are packed with numerous big stones and boulders which are practically unsuitable for any kind of cultivation. For this reason, previously most of the months of the year, the Juang of Keonjhar depended on jungle fruits, roots and tubers and also insects. But now after the inception of Juang Development Agency in Keonjhar district most of the Juang of Juangpirh have given up their traditional shifting cultivation and are now practising settled agriculture. They borrowed the knowledge of farming from neighbouring *Goura* caste and continue to do cultivation with the constant supply of agricultural implements and seeds by the JDA. The Juang as a whole are the worst sufferers to keep up the bare subsistence since their habitation in Juangpirh. JDA is trying to change their mind so that they can utilise modern agricultural implements for a better subsistence. It is interesting to note that they have started boro cultivation with high yielding varieties (HYV) provided by the agency. Paddy is usually cultivated by the Juang in the foothills where small streams and rivers flow.

Plough cultivation is also practised in those plots where river water is available and the JDA authority, i.e. *grass root manager*, is giving the idea about the necessities of plough and how to handle it. Getting the necessary instruction from the JDA, the Juang of Keonjhar are also practising ploughing, levelling, manuring, transplanting, weeding, harvesting and threshing for obtaining better crops from the agricultural fields.

The authorities of the JDA have alloted lands of different kinds to the Juang families and they are given individual ownership right on such lands. Community ownership right has been replaced by individual ownership. Altogether 114.45 acres of land has been distributed to the Juang by the JDA and average holding per land-owning household is 1.45 acres. About 40.62 acres Toila land has been given to the Juang by the JDA for a better socio-economic improvement as the Toila lands are suitable for rice, mustard and pulse cultivation. They are also cultivating potato, tobacco and papaya in their kitchen gardens. The seeds for the above are supplied by the LAMP on credit basis and after the harvesting the Juang recover their loan by giving the harvest crops. In the year, 1983-84, the Juang of the studied villages produced 320.95 quintals of different crops of which rice is 85.80 quintals and paddy is 152.13 quintals respectively.

Some livestock, such as bullock, goats and hens, were also given to the Juang by the JDA but most of them died by an epidemic disease which occurred in 1982-83, as reported by the informant. JDA has also taken initiative to advise the Juang to open saving accounts with the *Baitarani Grammya Bank*. As a result, some Juang have already opened savings account. This is a new kind of achievement for the JDA.

Approachable roads have been constructed by this agency which help in maintaining connected links with most of the Juang villages. As a result, the Juang of Juangpirh are attending the weekly market for selling firewood. The D.F.O. has given special permission to the Juang for collecting firewood from any reserved forest and the collection can be sold in the market days only. On the other hand, Juang could collect branches of Sal trees or other trees for making their huts. LAMP is primarily confined to extend credit facilities to the Juang and the credit is realised from them through purchasing of crops after harvest. LAMP also gives price support for their crops.

Educational Developmental Programme

Educational development is also linked up with social and economic development as it helps in removing illiteracy and ignorance. "The aim of tribal education should not be only the spreading literacy among the tribals but it should also enable these people to solve their socio-economic problems and improve their health condition" (Tripathi, 1970).

Altogether 20 villages have been adopted by the JDA and it has opened a *Gyanamandir* (preparatory school for the Juang children) in each of the adopted villages. The Juang parents send their children to these schools where *Gyananas*, teachers of these schools, are trying to improve child's general cleanliness alongwith preparatory education and also help them getting admitted into upper classes of the *Ashram* school. The Juang parents also send their children to nearby ashram school which is residential in nature. This significant change about educational aspiration has only occurred due to the constant efforts and motivation given by the agency. This success in making the children more conscious about the education was only possible by two factors: (1) the efficient planning and (2) by the execution and receptivity of the people for whom it is meant. As a result the literacy rate of the Juang has increased to 14.68% which itself indicates a healthy sign.

Health and Sanitation

Government has set up a health centre at Gonasika in order to provide necessary medical facilities to the Juang. The Government Health Centre and JDA's health personnel used to go house to house regularly for checking up and for clinical examination of the health of the people. At the time of the health personnel's visit if he finds that some one is affected by any disease, he immediately arranges to make a contact with the medical officer and also help by supplying the medicines free of cost. In Juangpirh, the people are usually affected by diarrhoea, dysentery, malaria and skin diseases. Now these diseases have been controlled to some extent by the JDA medical personnel. Sometimes the affected persons used to visit the health centre for doctor's consultation. As a result the total morbid condition has become less (72.07) pronounced compared to other tribal communities.

Disscussions

It may be mentioned here that the earlier life pattern of the Juang was well adapted to their immediate local environment. But due to a sudden trend of change resulting from the activities of JDA has in most cases caused to them a condition of psychological set back. This is because of the reason that they could neither go for acceptance of the programmes of JDA nor could they be inducted to the motivations of the JDA. It thus implies that certainly it is very necessary, rather a must, to appreciate and understand the life situation and culture of the Juang community prior to the implementation of any developmental scheme. The changes, which occurred due to the enthusiasms of JDA, are in the nature of showing interest to send their children to school and trying to maintain better health and sanitation habit. At the same time, it may be pointed out that some plans of the JDA either need reorientation or better be withdrawn, though the developmental schemes are being implemented by the executors despite various constraints.

Juang believe that land has not to be ploughed since it is their mother. Hence for farming they used to cut down trees and burn jungles to prepare as to be utilised as a manure. Successively after the natural rains they either plant saplings or sow seeds in the land. When the earth of the used land loses its fertility the Juang shift to the other land and practise the same. This is the common practice of the Juang. But when the JDA has forced the Juang for practising settled agriculture by supplying agricultural tools and implements alongwith high yielding seeds, most of the time they do not usually accept it fully for their subsistence. On the other hand, the agencies should take into cognizance of the reality of the family size of the

Juang, because it has a positive bearing with the kind of farming in terms of labour support. It was observed in the studied villages that the average household size is 4.44. And through shifting cultivation this limited number of heads could get support for their subsistence. But in settled agriculture more labour force is required and this again is related to economic system. Hence, we see that the apparent benefits of settled agriculture which become disadvantageous in the present case ought not to be imposed by JDA on the average small family size like Juang of Keonjhar.

So, special attention has been given by the JDA officials for educational programmes and for this the authority has set up a number of *Gyanamandir* in most of the adopted Juang villages. In each *Gyanamandir,* one *Gaynyama* or lady teacher is recruited for removing illiteracy. But in some cases *Ganyama* belongs to non-tribal community and for her it is very difficult to mix and convince the Juang parents and their children to get the idea about the importance of primary education. Sometimes the trained teacher and doctors are reluctant to stay in these remote tribal areas and as a result teachers are losing interest and the student fails to develop interest on education. Other factors also play a vital role in making the Juang children, non-interested in education. Most of the boys and girls usually go to the jungle for the collection of tubers, fruits and insects, etc. In various months of the year like February, March and May to August, children usually go for collection of forest products in the early morning and come back home in forenoon. Thus the school timings do not suit them. So economic need should be solved by maintaining a constant supply of free food to the school going children and also the timing of the school needs a suitable change. On the other hand JDA should make constant efforts, so that the Juang parents and children could realise the worth of education.

Juang are slowly accepting the allopathic medicines against their indigeneous herbal medicines. But the facilities for the allopathic treatment are not so adequate. The physicians should stay in the health centres. Due to the non-availability of doctor in Gonasika health centre the pregnant women and also the post delivery cases are not getting adequate medical help at the time of urgency. Similarly, the herbal medicines should be studied to identify their efficacy and remedial values by the agency's authorities.

Free and good medicines must be made available regularly and these should be distributed in the most interior areas, otherwise, Juang will lose their interest in modern allopathic medicines.

Basically, the Juang as a whole are very poor, although they are now enjoying benifits of changes in economy, education, health and sanitation due to the activities of the various agencies. But, for any tribal development direct involvement of social scientist at grass root level is a priority which cannot be compensated by mere submission and relating a research paper on development to cater only academic interest.

Acknowledgement

The author is grateful to DR. P.C. DUTTA, Superintending Anthropologist (P) of Anthropological Survey of India for giving valuable suggestions at the time of writing the final paper and to S.K. CHAUDHURY, for his kind co-operation.

INDEX